CULTURE
SHOCK!
Ireland

Patricia Levy

Graphic Arts Center Publishing Company
Portland, Oregon

In the same series

Australia	Indonesia	Spain	London at Your Door
Bolivia	Israel	Sri Lanka	Rome at Your Door
Borneo	Italy	Sweden	
Britain	Japan	Switzerland	A Globe-Trotter's Guide
Burma	Korea	Syria	A Student's Guide
California	Laos	Taiwan	A Traveller's Medical Guide
Canada	Malaysia	Thailand	A Wife's Guide
China	Mauritius	Turkey	Living and Working Abroad
Czech Republic	Morocco	United Arab	Working Holidays Abroad
Denmark	Nepal	Emirates	
France	Norway	USA	
Germany	Pakistan	USA—The South	
Greece	Philippines	Vietnam	
Hong Kong	Singapore		
India	South Africa		

Illustrations by TRIGG
Photographs by Danny Gralton
Patricia Levy and Sean Sheehan

© 1996 Times Editions Pte Ltd
Reprinted 1996, 1997

This book is published by special
arrangement with Times Editions Pte Ltd
Times Centre, 1 New Industrial Road, Singapore 536196
International Standard Book Number 1-55868-247-3
Library of Congress Catalog Number 95-79455
Graphic Arts Center Publishing Company
P.O. Box 10306 • Portland, Oregon 97296-0306 • (503) 226-2402

Printed in Singapore

AN IRISH BLESSING

May the road rise to meet you
May the wind be always at your back
May the sun shine warm upon you face
May the rains fall soft upon your fields
And, when we meet again
May God hold you in the palm of his hand.

CONTENTS

Map of Ireland   6
Preface   7

1 Paddies   9
2 A Terrible Beauty   22
3 A Load of Old Blarney   48
4 A Nation Once Again?   66
5 Moving Statues: Religion and National Identity   86
6 Money, Sex and Women   102
7 Irish Attitudes to Food and Drink   116
8 The Irish at Work   134
9 The Lure of the Land   152
10 Irish Solutions to Irish Problems   172
11 A Bit of Crack   188
12 Race, Creed or Colour   204
13 A Day at the Races   222
14 D.I.Y. Ireland   238

Cultural Quiz   264
Further Reading   270
The Author   277
Index   278

IRELAND

Ireland is the western most region of Europe and is comprised of 32 counties –
six of which are ruled by Britain and are referred to as Northern Ireland. The
other 26 form the Republic of Ireland which is politically autonomous.

PREFACE

The Irish people have spread themselves in great numbers across the world over the years and in doing so a strong impression of what it means to be Irish has developed. Many of the stereotypes which are connected to Ireland and her people are the product of a view of the Irish as immigrants, or else of a romantic notion of the 'Emerald Isle.'

On visiting and settling in Ireland you will find that many of these stereotypes are misplaced but often that they are borne of a certain truth, which you may at the time suspect the Irish are keen to nurture. Many of the idiosyncrasies of Irish life are at the root of the culture shock suffered by the newly arrived and it is learning to become a part of the Irish culture that offers the most rewarding challenge.

In recent years the 'Troubles' in Northern Ireland have largely overshadowed perceptions of the country as a whole and this, thankfully, has shown recent signs of changing. Ireland is a land steeped in history and tradition and these elements shape the lives of the Irish. *Culture Shock! Ireland* will give you an insight into the historical and political context in which modern Ireland exists, as well as practical advice on how to operate successfully in everyday situations.

Chapter One

PADDIES

There are no overall certitudes in Ireland any more. There's a lot of diversity of thinking, a lot of uncertainty, a lot of trying to assimilate to other cultures. It's a time when we need to take stock, to look into our hearts and find a sense of Irishness, to find a pride in ourselves that will make us sure of what we are.

—Mary Robinson
During her presidential campaign, 1990.

STEREOTYPES

So, here you are about to embark on the adventure of a lifetime, getting to know the Irish. Or perhaps you have already begun to do so and are looking for some guidance through the intricacies of the thought patterns and peculiar attitude to life you have encountered, or the labyrinth of attitudes to the horrors of the North. Let us begin, however, with what the Irish people are not – those terrible stereotypes that seem to stick to the Irish and label them in all corners of the world.

"Star Trek," the television science fiction series, started very humbly in the United States during the 1960s but is now firmly established as one of the most popular television programmes ever broadcast. It is shown across the world and is able to successfully communicate with audiences of different nationalities and ages. There were seven successive series of "Star Trek" and they became progressively more sophisticated as audiences warmed to the intelligent scripts relating the exploits of the captain and crew of a twenty-fourth century starship, the USS *Enterprise*. So, when in one episode of the sixth series, a colony of people are featured who speak with Irish accents, it is worth looking at the way these people are presented.

The USS *Enterprise* encounters a colony of people who have been abandoned on a far flung planet for generations. They now need rescuing and are brought aboard the *Enterprise* as a temporary safety measure. They all have stage Irish accents, wear peasant clothes, sleep alongside their animals, distil their own alcohol and play folk music on violins. The male members of the community leave all the work to the women, being more concerned with getting inebriated. They have little knowledge of even twentieth century culture, let alone the twenty-fourth century, and almost set the ship ablaze by kindling a fire out of sticks on one of the cargo decks. The leading woman is a fiery red head who berates all men and is characteristically presented with her sleeves rolled up and on her knees washing the floor. She bears more than a passing resemblance to the role played by Maureen O'Hara alongside John Wayne in *The Quiet Man*.

The captain's problem of what to do with this throwback to primitive Earth culture is fortuitously solved when the starship also encounters another colony. This community is characterised as effete and over-intellectual; they are highly scientific and have forgotten how to make babies the natural way and depend on a diminishing stock of clones to survive. They urgently require some new breeding stock in order to return to a natural system of reproduction and assured survival. The episode ends humorously with the captain able to successfully persuade the two colonies to unite and hopefully produce a new hybrid community, technologically advanced but also very earthy and human.

So, how many stereotypes did Captain Kirk and his crew on board the USS *Enterprise* manage to encounter in this representative group of Irish people?

The Drunken Irish Man

First we have the most potent stereotype of all, that singing staggering creature who holds up street lights, rifles the wife's purse for the price of his next stout, engages in comic street fights with his drinking buddy in which both of them miss their mark and fall over one another, and will do anything to get a free drink. This stereotyped image is the one that Americans most readily succumb to and it helps explain the cult status of John Ford's film, *The Quiet Man*, mentioned above. Despite the fact that Ford crafted better work, *The Quiet Man* is probably his most popular film. The village of Cong in County Mayo, where the film was made, thrives on the connection with the film and every year visitors to the place take guided tours and walks focusing on places that have a connection with the film. Among the many stereotypes traded on, the notion that Irish males have a natural predilection for alcohol is one that is steadfastly maintained through-out the film. A typical instance being the scene where a man's horse and cart, despite being driverless, comes to an abrupt halt outside the village pub.

Almost a cliche in itself this cut modern pub front in Limerick sets out to give the tourists confirmation of an imaginary rural Ireland.

The truth is that the Irish are not the world's heaviest drinkers. A recent survey of European drinking habits indicated that the British and Germans consume more alcohol per capita than the Irish. A possible explanation for the image of the hard-drinking Paddy lies in the experience of the expatriate Irishman living in a foreign place like England or New York and finding a pub to be one of the few places where he could socialise with his countrymen, as well as seeking solace in drink for what was often a very alienating existence.

What is true is that Ireland contains an unusually high number of pubs. Every town in Ireland – no matter how small and under-populated – seems to have more pubs than all the other shops put together. The only exception to this is in parts of the North where a staunch Protestant ethic has managed to exert a temperate influence on the proliferation of pubs.

The Simple Peasant

Then we have the type of stage Irishman who is too stupid to realise that you don't light fires on board the most technologically advanced starship of the twenty-fourth century. He has little understanding of anything more complex than his horse drawn plough and calls anything that looks remotely complicated a 'yoke.' His car is a wreck, held together by bits of string, he says 'begorrah' when confronted by a dishwasher or a computer, and he is the source of endless jokes. He also believes in leprechauns – the 'Little People.'

This is the Englishman's Irishman, or at least one of them. He works on building sites and spends the bulk of his working day leaning on his shovel discussing the shape of the hole he is making. The stereotype of the incredibly naive and stupid Irishman may share its roots with those that helped create the image of the equally simple minded Pole in the United States. In both cases there was the phenomenon of thousands of country men and women emigrating from a rural culture into the industrial cities of foreign countries. Confronted with a relatively advanced technology there was a natural tendency for the newcomer to feel and behave as if in awe of the new and modern. This actively encouraged an attitude of superiority on the part of those more familiar with the trappings of Western society.

The Gift of the Gab

Then we have the Irish man who spends his days weaving stories, fluidly oiling social relations through mere words, tricking information out of his unsuspecting conversation partner, somehow making nonsense take on a meaning. Queen Elizabeth I of England is credited with having introduced a new word into the language as a result of being on the receiving end of this innate capacity to charm through talk. As the ruler of sixteenth century Ireland she wanted Lord Blarney to give up his extensive lands to her as many other clan leaders had done. In return he would be allowed to lease back his lands from her and would be free from any threat from her armies.

Unwilling for obvious reasons to comply but equally unwilling to refuse her, he procrastinated. Receiving yet another humble but noncommittal letter from him she is said to have declared that the letter was a 'load of old blarney,' or words to that effect.

Visitors to Blarney Castle in County Cork kiss a particular stone in the castle's wall that has the reputation of being able to confer, in return, the gift of the gab. The Irish apparently require no such magic, being blessed it seems with a natural talent for elegant fluency and smooth talk. The best English in the world is reputed to be spoken in Dublin and Irish writers, for instance, make up a sizeable proportion of required reading for undergraduates studying English in universities not only in England but all over the world. It is also true that listening to the bantering of Irish conversation – its relaxed rhythm and easy way with words – the English person with their clearly defined meanings and formal politeness can often be left feeling clumsy and humourless.

The ability to talk easily to strangers is very noticeable in Ireland and stems from a genuine curiosity about other people. Unlike many cultures which go to great lengths to not have to recognise the existence of another person in certain situations, the Irish consider their day a success if they have chatted to a foreigner or someone from another part of Ireland who can tell them about the weather or the strange doings of foreign parts or people. This can be very frustrating at times to outsiders, queuing up at a check-out in a supermarket and delayed by interminable conversations between customers and the till operator.

An explanation for the fluidity and fluency of spoken English in Ireland may be found in the fact that Irish English is simply different to Standard English. It was not until the nineteenth century that Gaelic lost ground to the cultural hegemony of the British empire and, while the imposition of the English language was pervasive and permanent, there is reason to think that the deep roots of Gaelic syntax and style left their mark on the way the new language was spoken.

Also relevant is the fact that Ireland did not develop into a modern capitalist state at the same pace as the rest of western Europe. Due to English rule, Ireland was the only country that underwent a process of de-industrialisation during the nineteenth century, and even today Ireland remains an essentially rural society. Small towns proliferate, the face behind the counter in a shop or supermarket is likely to be familiar, people have more time to take matters in their stride and this all contributes to a way of life where talking is more than a mere function. A conversation, even to a relative stranger while engaged in a commercial transaction, becomes a social act. This is especially so among the older generation who have often grown up with an oral tradition.

The Virago

And who looks after all these Irish men? The flaming red head of course. When young she is a beauty, fierce in her loyalties and her mockery of all men, but when she falls for a man he'd better beware. She has stood – arms akimbo – in many an American movie, giving out to the world and his brother. She leads her husband a dog's life, constantly curbing his drinking, nagging him to work harder, cleaning the house and getting the best she can afford for her growing brood of children. She accepts the guidance of the Catholic Church with blind faith, vets her sons' future wives with an eagle eye, disposing quickly of those who will not meet her standards. She finds good jobs and eventually husbands for her daughters and is a tower of strength until the day she slips quietly away in the huge bed in which she gave birth to her many children. Her last glance on earth is at the crucifix which hangs above her bed as it has done all her life.

This is a fading stereotype, due probably to its origins in a past era when moral certainties and the power of the church endorsed aspects of the role. In the past, too, economic hardships and the fact that women were not encouraged to seek employment outside the home allowed the image of the Irish woman as virago to flourish.

The Villainous Gunman

The demonised IRA man – the merciless killer with hate in his heart – has a predictable image in Britain's media. He is usually portrayed as being in his mid twenties, wearing a green jacket with a balaclava over his face and a black beret. He has lived all his life among violence, acquiring his early urban guerilla skills as a teenager throwing stones at the security forces. His religion plays second fiddle to his sense of misguided nationality, the reality of which is seen to be a vicious tribalism that only results in the deaths of innocent civilians. The hard men of violence in Ireland were commonly bracketed in the popular imagination alongside ruthless Palestinian terrorists. The IRA man has been consistently presented to the public – particularly in Britain, the main forum for IRA attacks, – as irredeemably evil, a heartless monster with no inkling of mercy or pity in his heart.

A difficulty with this stereotype is that three out of ten nationalists in the North vote for Sinn Féin, the political wing of the IRA, at elections. In October 1993 thousands turned out to attend the funeral of Thomas Begley, an IRA man who blew himself up when the bomb he was carrying went off prematurely and killed nine innocent people in Belfast. His coffin was carried by Gerry Adams, the president of Sinn Féin and a man closely associated with the IRA, who as such had once been elected as a Member of Parliament in Westminster. The stereotype is deconstructed not in the least by the fact that a significant number of ordinary people in Northern Ireland consistently vote for a party that sees the IRA's position as very understandable.

The Fighting Mick

The image of the villainous gunman fits easily alongside the stereotype of the Irish as naturally prone to violence. This perception is readily embodied on the enormously popular television soap opera "Coronation Street" which is also screened in Ireland. The character's name is Jim, he has red hair, drinks rather too much and uses his fists instead of his brain. At heart he is a kindly man who just wants to be loved. He has a simple set of values, loves his family but has trouble expressing his feelings. As such, he is misunderstood, easily manipulated into losing his temper and always contrite afterwards.

The Wily Dubliner

A more recent addition to the family of Irish men is the artful Dubliner. He has a vocabulary that would turn the air blue, pronounces 'book' as 'buke,' avoids work as much as possible and is cynical about everything. He has little regard for business or making money, although he'd accept it if it was given to him. He is embodied for the Irish in a puppet called Dustin who appears on Irish children's television. Dustin is a turkey, works as a refuse collector, is completely incoherent and during the 1992 General election stood unofficially on a platform of 'bringing the DART (the Dublin subway system) to Dingle' (one of the western-most spots in the south of Ireland). He got air time on the national news as well as several thousand votes.

Paddies, Micks, Colleens and so on

The stereotypes roll on: the local priest who is well able to take his drink and turns a blind eye to minor infringements of the law by his parishioners; the New York policeman; the tight-lipped spinster; the barefoot urchin; the chinless Anglo-Irish lord of the manor. Then there's the slick local politician doling out kickbacks and making sure government contracts and European Union subsidies go where they can garner political support.

Why is it that of all nations in the world there so many comic and often unkind images of the Irish? Perhaps the nature of an Irish identity facilitates caricature and generalisation. Unlike other western European countries, the United States or South East Asia, while Ireland has been a place that people have left it has rarely, until very recently, been one where new groups come searching for a better life. Like Japan or mainland China it has never benefited from the influx of new ideas or other cultures, the people have never had to deal with issues of racism, for instance, and has only in the recent past discovered sexism. It is uniformly white, Christian, and conservative in nature. A mono-culture invites labelling, for national traits are easily identified, and when Irishness is exported to other countries by emigrants it is subject to examination and often ridicule. Paradoxically the number of people proudly claiming Irish descent, however tenuous their connection may be, is testament to the widely held perception of Irish charm and wide acceptance of the Irish.

One reason for the pervasiveness of the stereotypes is probably the massive emigration of the Irish to all corners of the world. Like most other immigrant groups, they have created small enclaves of their own culture in foreign places and inevitably this invites caricature by the dominant host culture.

It is true however – and this is common to most stereotypes – that there is an element of truth in these images of the Irish. The simple peasant may belong to Ireland's recent past but there is a rather self conscious element of him even in modern Dublin, thank goodness.

The Irish have an ability to take things easy even in the fastest city centre. This often disguises itself as a naive wonder at all things modern.

REAL IRISH ICONS

So what are the Irish really like and what motivates their behaviour and feelings? Despite the many problems Ireland has, economically, politically and perhaps socially, the Irish have an amazing capacity to see the humorous side of events both in Ireland and abroad. In 1992, at the same time as controversy raged over the availability of condoms, the story broke that Bishop Casey, the bishop of Galway and a notable public figure, had an illegitimate teenage son and was paying off his mother with church funds. Within days, T-shirts appeared on the streets of Dublin bearing the words: 'Wear a Condom, Just in Casey.'

Just what is it about the Irish that gives them the ability to see the funny side of things in a country where some of the laws still reflect a fading moral code; where, for example, the possibility of divorce is still being debated and where homosexuality was a crime until 1993. What are the Irish like, once the superficial layers of the stereotypes are peeled away?

The Past

First of all, Ireland's present state is irrevocably bound to its mostly tragic past. Like any country that has provided an arena for colonisation, Ireland needs time to recover from the depredations of its colonial past. This recovery is severely inhibited by the fact that the problem of the North is still not settled. Like many other countries Ireland was colonised in a greedy and brutal way and had to fight to remove its colonial masters. Unlike other countries, it happens to be parked right next door to its erstwhile imperial rulers and six counties of Ireland are still a part of Britain.

The following chapter is devoted to Ireland's history, showing how the past haunts the present. It will help explain how intrinsically Irish it is that the country's most popular chat show can focus on a new biography of a politician who has been dead for thirty years, with members of the audience earnestly questioning the biographer about aspects of his subject's life.

Change is in the Air

There are no two ways about it, the times they are changing in Ireland and in many ways women are at the forefront. There is an exciting sense that women are rediscovering the power that they once had in Ireland's dim past. The most popular Irish national figure of modern times is Mary Robinson. She has sure-footedly taken a defunct, not to say, dull job – that of a non-executive and mostly ceremonial presidency – and made it a showcase for a sense of Irish dignity and liberal-mindedness. More women were elected to the Dáil, the country's parliament, in 1992 than at any other time and more Irish women represent their country of under three million in the Dáil than British women represent their country of over 50 million.

Linked with this emergence of women's voices are various scandals in the political and social sphere that have left people with a sense that too much has been let slide for too long. The country is more open to change than at any time in the past and the Irish are dealing with it in a characteristically humane way.

Ireland has much to offer an overpopulated and increasingly unstable Europe and the Irish, with their relaxed sense of life and innate good humour, attract an increasing number of visitors each year, many of whom choose to stay on permanently despite the violence of the North. An ancient country where civilisation flourished while the rest of Europe was sunk in barbarism – Ireland and the Irish are about due to come back into their own.

Chapter Two

A TERRIBLE BEAUTY

And what if excess of love
Bewildered them till they died?
I write it out in a verse –
MacDonagh and MacBride
And Connolly and Pearse
Now and in time to be,
Wherever green is worn,
All changed, changed utterly:
A terrible beauty is born.
        —W. B. Yeats, *Easter 1916*

HISTORY

Why, it may be asked, in a book dedicated to explaining some of the peculiarities of modern Ireland, is it necessary to transport oneself back in time several centuries? Why not just cut to the modern details without bothering to unravel their historical origins? Ireland's present is bound up in its past in a way that cannot be compared to most other countries and its people have a feeling for history that informs and shapes their consciousness. Other countries have histories of invasion from which they freed themselves and started over but Ireland isn't so simple. As Brendan Behan (1923–64) the noted writer and political activist put it: "Other people have a nationality. The Irish and the Jews have a psychosis."

The Mythical History

Ireland's history effortlessly mixes the mythical with the modern. Look into any school history text in Ireland and you'll find Celtic heroes engaged in battles with the gods, being turned into swans or disembarking from their boats to bivouac on the back of a sleeping giant whale for a few days. The story of St. Patrick casting out all the snakes from Ireland is just as likely to be in primary school history books as in religious texts. The fusing of history and myth runs through Irish history and is stronger in the twentieth century than in most other periods.

There is a cultivated and sophisticated myth that one Irish leader, Eamon De Valera, literally rode to power in the 1930s by arriving at open air meetings on horseback wearing a great cape and broad brimmed hat, 'illuminated by blazing sods of turf, and casting spells in bad Irish' as the writer of the *Begrudger's Guide to Irish Politics* put it. Many of the wall murals in Derry and Belfast deliberately set out to create just such a romantic mythical image for the women and men they portray. It isn't that the Irish are too simple to appreciate the difference between myth and reality but rather that they view reality in a self-consciously different way.

If you visit any small country community in Ireland the sense of history can be intense. My own grandfather-in-law happily told stories about a family member who was thrown from a horse at a certain spot resulting in a broken neck. He told the story as if he had witnessed it, but on questioning it turned out the event had happened in the last century. Another elderly relative in County Mayo showed me the field where Michael Davitt held one of the first Land League meetings, and pointed out a large stone in a nearby field which marked the burying ground of a French soldier – part of a force dispatched by Napoleon to join an Irish revolt – who had died of natural causes in 1798.

Many small towns have their historical society attended by quite average people who think nothing of spending an afternoon wandering about the hillsides examining signs of Bronze Age habitation. The fields of Ireland are dotted with the remains of pre-Christian society and in County Kerry some of the structures are sufficiently intact to be used as tool-sheds or grain-stores by farmers about to step into the twenty-first century. Farmers cheerfully plough around standing stones and circular forts, dating back millennia, that they are too superstitious or respectful of to move out of their way. To the Irish, history is continuous with the present in a way that is rarely understood in British or American society.

In the field next to my house is the unmarked grave of a woman who died in the Famine of 1845–49, set at the side of the field so that no valuable farming land would be lost. In the field behind my house are clearly visible potato ridges last cultivated well over a hundred years ago. My nearest neighbour was called Din-Long-Dinny, from Dennis (his own first name) and then Long Dennis, after his tall father. Another neighbour was known as Jack-Tom-Ned, from his own real first name, Jack, and his father, Tom, and his grandfather, Ned. This way there was no chance of confusing Jack-Tom-Ned with the many other Jacks in the neighbourhood, or the presumably smaller number of Jack-Tom personages.

Standing stones are usually aligned with the summer or winter solstice and are believed to have had a religious significance for the Celtic tribes of Ireland.

So, for a people who revere the past and have this strong oral tradition that draws their grandparents and great grandparents into their daily lives, the events of modern Irish history are all the more tragic. At the same time it may well be that this tradition of keeping history close to the present is largely what prevents the Irish from overcoming these events.

Culturally speaking, the Irish are not a people who can put the past behind them and still be Irish and anyone wanting to understand the Irish needs at least a nodding acquaintance with some of the crucial epochs of the past. Understanding the situation in Northern Ireland is only the most obvious example of the need to acknowledge the events of centuries past. Ireland has a rich history and a specific knowledge of its development is in itself a topic of great interest. More generally, understanding Ireland and the Irish people depends on a knowledge of history.

Land of Saints and Scholars

A good place to start is in the seventh and eighth centuries for, while the rest of Europe was sinking into the Dark Ages, Ireland's society was a beacon of civilisation.

In Ireland Christianity had taken a strong hold but had developed along curiously Irish lines. A legal system which protected the rights of the individual and in particular women, regulated secular life while ecclesiastical centres like Armagh led the known world in literature, history and science. Scholars travelled to Ireland from all over Europe to study at the feet of the masters and Irish missionaries travelled around Europe converting the heathens of Switzerland, Spain, France and even England. The Vikings carried away Irish artifacts to copy, and trade flourished. All around the coasts of Ireland tiny communities of monks made exquisite religious manuscripts, some of which have somehow found their way into foreign museums. Clans protected their own people, elected their leaders and women could hold as important a place in their clan as men. Communal hospitals existed, each tribe traditionally sheltered passing strangers and the law – known as Brehon Law – laid down rules for arbitration and compensation in disputes over land or behaviour.

Invasion

In time, the English incursion into Ireland changed everything. Ecclesiastical centres were deliberately destroyed, the Gaelic language was made illegal, intermarriage between the Irish and their invaders banned and Catholics were forbidden to enter walled cities, own land or any other property over a set amount. Families were encouraged to betray one another by laws offering younger sons or even wives their family's land if they would convert to Protestantism.

The first serious wave of invaders were the Anglo-Normans, the sons and grandsons of the men who invaded England with William the Conqueror in 1066. The Normans built walled cities, encouraged trade and generally learned to live in close harmony with the people whose lands they had taken. They discovered the benefits of the Brehon system of law and gradually the two cultures intermingled, Norman sons took Gaelic wives as rival lords and clan leaders made pacts with one another. Between them the Anglo-Normans and Irish lords evolved a legal system and system of government which represented and benefited all Irish people. Everyone prospered.

At the same time, around the twelfth and thirteenth centuries, there was a Gaelic revival; literature flourished, patronised both by the Norman and Gaelic lords. The Third Earl of Desmond, an Anglo-Irish lord and the head of the English colony in Ireland wrote excellent

Ancient stones with carved faces. This one on White Island shows a bishop's mitre, indicating that it dates back to early Christian times.

Gaelic poetry. The children of English lords married to Gaelic women grew up speaking Gaelic. This assimilation can be seen nowadays in some of the Irish names. The name Burke, common in Connaught, was originally De Burgh and to counteract this process of assimilation the English government enacted laws designed to halt it in the Statutes of Kilkenny, introducing a system of apartheid. The English part of Ireland grew smaller and smaller as the Normans became assimilated or left, until the area around Dublin known as the Pale was all that was left. (Hence the expression 'beyond the pale' for an area beyond control.)

As the centuries progressed English kings, at war with both Europe and Scotland and desperate to bring Ireland under control, sent armies against the Gaelic and Norman lords until the Tudors finally got enough cash together to make a real attempt. Henry VIII's break from Rome had established Protestantism in England and Catholic Ireland promised rich pickings. Apart from the rich monasteries which existed throughout Ireland, the forests would provide the raw material for the shipbuilding industry that was so vital to England's political and mercantile power. In addition, the oak trees that covered the country were turned into charcoal for smelting ores. Ireland's resources were as economically important to England as Middle East oil is today.

The Plantation

By the end of the sixteenth century, under the reign of Queen Elizabeth, the process known as the Plantation began in earnest; throwing Norman and Gael alike off their land, and their peasants with them. They were replaced with fortified houses with new English landlords occupying them and loyal Protestant working people under their command. Whole towns were built along English lines and a typical example was Bandon in County Cork that carried a notice on the walls proclaiming:

> Jew, Turk or atheist
> May enter here, but not a papist

A reply soon appeared stating that:

> Whoever wrote this wrote it well
> For the same is written in the gates of Hell

From the seventeenth century onwards the Plantation was particularly prevalent in the eight counties of the north of Ireland, traditionally known as Ulster, but resistance here by the indigenous Irish was proving troublesome. The English decided upon a policy of continuing and extending the Plantation and completely replacing the native population. Settlers from the lowlands of Scotland were brought into Ulster in huge numbers. In 1607, unable to fight the English off but unwilling to submit, some ninety or more of the leading nobles of Ulster left Ireland for the continent. This event – the Flight of the Earls – has become a part of the myth building process of Irish history.

After the Flight of the Earls the way was open for large scale confiscation and redistribution of property. The land was divided into two-thousand acre plots and rented to new settlers who were obliged to subdivide and rent out again to Protestant tenants. These people were by tradition arable farmers rather than pastoral ones and they brought their own strong traditions and lifestyle. A number of Catholics remained in the area because not enough Protestants could be found and they remained for the most part labourers, without land and alienated from their neighbours.

Outside of Northern Ireland, the brutal process of British cultural imperialism is closely associated with Oliver Cromwell's brief reign. Terrible retribution fell upon the entire populations of Drogheda and Wexford and those events too have entered the folk memory of Ireland in a way that earlier savageries carried out during Elizabeth's reign did not. Cromwell's changes left the peasantry in their place but altered the nature of the landed gentry completely from largely Catholic to wholly Protestant. By 1660 Catholics could only own land west of the River Shannon, in Connaught and County Clare. Between Connaught and Ulster the new landlords were devout Protestants, many of whom had fought for Cromwell in his subjugation of the country.

The Battle of the Boyne

After Cromwell the monarchy was restored in England and dispossessed Catholics viewed with hope the accession of the Catholic James I to the throne in 1685. But English Protestants grew gradually more and more wary of his religious inclinations and the implications for the ruling aristocracy in England. William of Orange, married to James' protestant daughter, was invited to take over the crown. James fled first to France and then to Ireland where he set up a parliament in exile. It reversed the land settlements of Cromwell giving back all land confiscated from Catholics. It also declared that the property of anyone supporting William was confiscated.

For a brief spell Ireland became a theatre of war played out between the rival powers of Europe. Due to a series of political alliances James had the support of France and the Irish, while William had the Holy Roman Empire and Spain, both Catholic states, as his allies. For the Irish the battle was between the older inhabitants of the land and the new settlers and the two sides were evenly balanced.

Visit any Protestant town in the North around July 12th and the major battles will be laid out before you in colourful street murals and embroidered banners. First was the siege of Derry in 1690, when the city was saved from the Catholics by the foresight of some apprentice boys who ran to shut the gates just in time. In the same year the two kings met in battle at the Boyne river where 36,000 Williamite troops faced an opposition of 25,000 men across the river. It was a hard fought battle lasting many hours and led to James' retreat in flight with his army relatively unharmed but a victory for the Williamites of great psychological and strategic importance.

All of Ireland as far south as Dublin fell to the Williamite army while James fell back south of the Shannon. Limerick became the scene for another fierce confrontation which has also entered the Irish psyche. When the Treaty of Limerick was signed in 1691 it gave Irish soldiers the freedom to leave for France and 14,000 men – christened the Wild Geese – left forever. The defenders of Limerick were guaranteed their property and the right to continue their professions but the terms of the treaty were systematically reneged on. Within a short time, the Catholic share of the land of Ireland was reduced to about one seventh of the total.

The Penal Laws

After the departure of the Wild Geese the Irish Parliament became entirely Protestant and all Catholics were forced to pay a tithe to the Church of Ireland while Irish trade was heavily restricted. A Catch 22 situation had arisen. The rulers of Ireland were a largely imported minority dependant on England for their continued domination of

31

Limerick Castle where the Treaty of Limerick was signed between William of Orange and the Catholics.

Ireland. They had to do what England said even if it meant that their own livelihoods were damaged. Unlike the Anglo-Normans these new Planters had no common ground with the native Irish and it was in their interests to maintain the system of apartheid. This system now began to be enforced in a series of laws which came to be known as the Penal Laws. They were justified by the very real threat of returning Irish Catholic mercenaries then fighting in Europe, and the news of persecution of Huguenots and other Protestant groups in other parts of Europe.

In effect the Penal Laws were only enforced in areas where it was felt necessary to keep Catholics out of the ruling hierarchy. All professions had to take an oath of loyalty to the Protestant religion, as did commissioned officers and Members of Parliament. The other area where Catholics could gain power was in the ownership of land

and so laws were passed prohibiting Catholics from buying land or taking long leases. Many big landowners and professionals like lawyers, for whom class privilege and property rights were always more important than religion, converted to Protestantism. Gradually the number of Catholics owning land fell until by 1778 only 5% of land was Catholic owned.

It is debatable whether the very real economic supremacy enjoyed by Protestants, while undoubtedly detrimental to Catholic men of property, made the life of Irish peasants much poorer or deprived than it would have been under Catholic landlords. But the mythologising and at times masochistic gloss that is given to Irish history has encouraged a simplistic picture to be drawn of the poor Catholic peasant downtrodden by the nasty Protestants. A good example is that while Catholic priests were technically outlawed under the Penal Laws the priesthood was, nevertheless, generally tolerated and ignored except in times of national security. Most large towns and all the cities had Catholic chapels, small primitive structures but nonetheless there for all to see. It remained in the interests of the Protestant minority to keep the peasants as Catholics, otherwise what ground could they have for keeping them in a state of poverty? Indeed, nonconformist Protestant groups got no kinder treatment from the established Protestant ruling classes than did the Catholics. It was less a question of religious belief and more an economic and class issue. Nonetheless, around Ireland today can be seen signs pointing to mass-rocks where dedicated men of the cloth were supposed to have conducted masses in secret, oblivious to their personal safety. It is more likely that these mass-rocks simply served rural communities that did not have the benefit of a church building.

The Penal Laws were repealed in 1778 and 1782 and Catholics became landowners on a quite considerable scale. When a movement did emerge at the end of the eighteenth century calling for Irish rights, it was led by a Protestant.

Agitation and Rebellion

Wolfe Tone was a Protestant who helped found the United Irishmen, a movement calling for a reformed Irish Parliament that would campaign for an end to the trade restrictions and unite all Irish people of both religions. He sought help from revolutionary France, then at war with England, and a French fleet carrying 14,000 men set out for Ireland but was scattered by bad weather and failed to make a landing. In 1798 open rebellion broke out around Dublin, Wexford and Waterford in the south and Antrim and Down in the North. The rebels were defeated within four months, Wolf Tone was arrested and later committed suicide.

The rebellion was followed by the 1801 Act of Union which abolished the Irish Parliament and made Ireland a part of Britain. Constitutionally, matters remained like this until 1921 but the intervening years are packed with tales of rebellion, heroic leaders and tragic martyrs – the very stuff of Irish legend and song that forms an integral part of contemporary Irish culture. A look at one of the heroes, Daniel O'Connell, shows how nationalist hero-worship can so easily simplify complex historical events.

The Great Liberator?

Catholics could own land and they could vote but were barred from sitting as Members of Parliament in Westminster. It was Daniel O'Connell's achievement to successfully spearhead a national campaign for the abolition of this restriction in 1829. He did not, as is commonly supposed, win the right of Catholics to vote and when he went on to campaign for the repeal of the Act of Union – not national independence but the restoration of an Irish Parliament – he took pains to express loyalty to the British Crown. What was being sought was an Irish Parliament that would govern affairs as part of Britain.

By the 1840s O'Connell was leading a mass movement in support of repeal of the Act of Union, holding 'monster meetings' throughout Ireland where hundreds of thousands of people turned out to hear him speak. Finally the English government banned one of the meetings, due to be held at Clontarf, and O'Connell called off the meeting. The momentum had been lost and before nationalism found a new voice the tragedy of the Famine was inflicted on Ireland.

O'Connell failed in his attempt. What he did do was enter that specially Irish realm of mythical heroism where all weaknesses are forgiven and blemishes disappear. While he did undeniably help create a national consciousness, he was not prepared to confront British power and when it came to the crunch he knuckled under and went quietly home to Kerry where he had extensive property. His unwillingness to square up to British power led to a split within the movement and another group emerged, willing to contemplate violence against the English.

After Irish independence, the main thoroughfare of Dublin, called Sackville Street at the time, was renamed O'Connell Street.

The Famine

In the 1845 census, Ireland's population stood at 8.5 million. In 1851, three years after the Famine, it was 6.5 million. A million people had died of hunger or associated diseases such as dysentery, typhus and cholera and another million had left for America in the coffin ships, so called because around one fifth of their passengers died during their journey to the United States. While the Famine was a natural disaster like an earthquake or tidal wave it is glaringly obvious that the disaster was made worse by English policy in Ireland.

Population had been increasing during the eighteenth and nineteenth centuries as the peasant farmers turned more and more to growing wheat as a cash crop to pay the rent and depending almost wholly for food on the potato, a vegetable which will not store well. England had maintained trade barriers preventing the Irish economy developing and forcing the increasing population to depend on farming for an income. When the potato crop failed in 1845 it spelt disaster.

While the peasants starved to death there were excellent harvests of other crops like wheat but these were strictly for export. Some landlords tried their best for their tenants but the attitudes of many resulted in tenant evictions, putting responsibility for them on the workhouses. Even the efforts to help made the situation worse. Poor relief was given in return for work and all over Ireland today 'Famine roads' can be seen – roads built for no other reason than to provide work for starving men whose pay was unable to provide them with enough calories for the next day's work. The soup given out in soup kitchens bloated stomachs but provided little sustenance to the growing number of starving people. The crowded conditions in the workhouses led to epidemics which were responsible for even more deaths.

The consequences of the Famine were enormous. Until 1847 the typical economic unit was about five acres or less of land supporting one large family. After the evictions the typical farm was up to thirty acres. Emigration became the norm and there was enormous resentment against England for the way it had handled the disaster and even greater hostility between tenant and landlord.

The nationalist John Mitchell (1815–75) lived through the famine and recorded the event in his *Jail Journal*; "... families, when all was eaten and no hope left, took their last look at the sun, built up their cottage doors, that none might see them die nor hear their groans, and were found weeks afterwards, skeletons on their own hearth."

Folk memory of those days is still strong in Ireland. On the positive side the Irish give generously to Third World famine appeals perhaps as a result of the empathy they feel but there is still a lingering sense of resentment against the English and the descendants of the landed gentry. The Irish who made a new life in the United States carried with them their bitterness and established a tradition of financing independence struggles in 'the old country.'

Home Rule

The years after the Famine were spent for the most part just surviving but as conditions improved tenant farmers began a drive to get security of tenure, fair rents and the right to sell the tenancy. The Land League was founded by Michael Davitt and others. At the same time a nationalist movement was burgeoning but it wasn't until the two movements combined under the leadership of Charles Stewart Parnell and Michael Davitt that real changes were forced out of the British government. The struggle between the landlords and tenants grew increasingly violent and it was during these years that the term boycott entered the language. Captain Boycott was a land agent in County Mayo whose neighbours refused to harvest the crops of the farms whose tenants he had evicted. Such a policy of ostracism had been urged by the Land League and it proved an effective weapon.

Parnell, Davitt and other leaders spent much time in prison and the Land League was run by women, led by Parnell's sister. Eventually, by a series of acts of parliament, tenants were given the right to buy their farms with state aid. These were hard-won gains but the British were again using the divide and rule technique by giving one element of the opposition what it wanted while denying the long term desire for independence. Gladstone, leader of the Liberal Party at Westminster, had meanwhile begun to support the cause of Irish Home Rule. Ireland would still be part of the British Empire but with its own parliament. Gladstone's efforts to implement this plan split the Liberal Party in England and he subsequently lost power. In addition the scandal of Parnell's affair with a married woman lost him the support of the church and further divided the Home Rule movement.

The Celtic Twilight

As the movement lost momentum in the 1870s it was replaced in the last twenty years of the nineteenth century by the Gaelic Revival, a somewhat dilettante movement which was largely Protestant and literary at first but met its political counterpart in the Gaelic League, founded in 1893. Gaelic sports were encouraged and in some cases invented, the language was taught in evening classes and Gaelic dress revived. Nationalism is often accompanied by a narrow-minded mentality and the patriotic propaganda of the Celtic Twilight, as it became known, was deservedly mocked by writers like James Joyce – who rechristened it the "Cultic Twalette" – and Flann O'Brien. Viewed more sympathetically, the Irish were fighting the cultural imperialism of the British who portrayed them in their cartoons as ignorant apes. The Irish were determined to create their own images of themselves and to this period belongs the beginning of the process of mythologising the past and fusing history with legend.

The Gaelic Revival's program of cultural reawakening took on political overtones. It became the beginning of a claim for complete independence in a country that no-one had really regarded as a separate culture from Britain for years. The argument went that where there was a separate culture and language then, by rights, a separate nation should exist. Political groups allied themselves with the aims and aspirations of the Gaelic Revival and a new and far stronger nationalist movement developed to challenge their non-Celtic rulers.

In the early years of the twentieth century the Gaelic League flourished and linked many politically active groups. Also the Industrial Revolution had finally arrived in Ireland and a new underfed, poorly housed working class had emerged in the slums of Dublin. Karl Marx considered Dublin to be one of the places most likely to spark off world revolution. New heroes emerged as women like Constance Markeivicz and trade unionists and socialists like Jim Larkin and James Connolly found common cause with mystical nationalists like Patrick Pearse.

A great lockout strike in the capital in 1913 further united and galvanised the disparate groups who were now forming into citizens' armies and training in the streets of Dublin. Things were different now from what they had ever been. This wasn't a disparate group of men with their own limited and selfish ends but rather a politically idealistic movement which cut across class, religion and gender. What it lacked in numerical support it made up for in republican rhetoric and commitment.

The Easter Rising

The Easter Rising of 1916 continues to fill an ambiguous role in the Irish consciousness although it was never a serious attempt to militarily destroy British power. About 1,600 members of the two citizens' militias operating in Ireland turned out in Dublin and the General Post Office – until then a building without any symbolic status – was occupied as the headquarters of the rebels. If the rebels had been seriously planning a coup d'état they might have planned to occupy Dublin Castle, the British headquarters, instead of a municipal building in the city's main shopping area. The rising failed, as many of its perpetrators knew it would, but out of their failure they hoped a new breed of Celtic warriors would emerge.

The initial response by Dubliners was disconcerting. The rebels were ignored and later derided and pelted with fruit when led away as prisoners. The only community support was in the form of looting by dispossessed Dubliners taking advantage of the chaos. However, the savage way in which the leaders of the rebellion were treated, fifteen of whom were executed, including James Connolly who was wounded in the ankle and, unable to stand, faced the firing squad tied to a chair, swung public opinion all over the world behind the Irish cause. This in turn created a focus for the Irish themselves and by its end many more people considered Irish independence a possibility, although few thought that it could be achieved by constitutional means. In the 1918 elections that marked the end of the First World War the Irish nationalist party, Sinn Féin, gained the vast bulk of the Irish seats and formed its own Irish Parliament, the Dáil Eireann in Dublin. There was to be no more truck with the Westminster Parliament and the old constitutionalists who had campaigned on behalf of Irish nationalism were relegated to the dustbin of history.

To talk of Irish history as a myth building process is not to derogate events or to deny their existence. The men and women who fought in the 1916 uprising were asserting Ireland's claim to be independent and the idea that Ireland only meant 26 counties and excluded most of Ulster would have struck them as ludicrous. When Irish independence was conceded in 1921, minus six counties in the north, the aspirations of Easter 1916 remained unfulfilled. To this day they are still unfulfilled and this is what accounts for the continuing fascination with events in Dublin in 1916 which, at the time, were largely met with indifference by the majority of Dubliners. The young man who in October 1993 was blown to pieces as he carried a bomb into a fish and chip shop in the Shankill Road in Belfast, taking innocent men women and children with him, had a picture of the 1916 Rising on the wall over his bed. The bomb had exploded prematurely and was intended only for loyalist terrorists. It is interesting that the statue in the General Post office in Dublin which commemorates the Rising depicts not Connolly or Pearse, or any of the other martyrs, but Cu Chullain the mythical Irish hero.

Any seismologist mapping the psychological fault lines of modern Ireland has good reason to draw attention to Easter 1916. Yeats, writing very soon after the event, captured the moment in his poetry but could hardly guess how it would still disturb the national consciousness nearly a century later. While the Rising prepared the way for the independence struggle that would see Ireland emerge as a separate nation it also asserted a claim that the IRA and Sinn Féin continue to struggle for – a united and independent Ireland of 32 counties. Contemporary Irish leaders want to be seen as worthy representatives of their country but they have no wish to continue the struggle that the rebels of 1916 died for. It is often possible to discern a deep unease in Irish citizens of the Republic about the question of the North and the source of this unease lies, to a large extent, in their repression of the unfinished business begun by the heroes of 1916.

The Anglo-Irish War

The violent struggle for independence lasted from 1919 to 1921 and was characterised by guerilla warfare on the part of the insurrectionists and consequent reprisals and executions by the British troops. The worst atrocities were committed by ex-soldiers who were enrolled as special constables and named the 'Black and Tans' due to the colour of their uniform. Their excesses ranged from beatings and murders to the ransacking of whole towns and the burning of Cork City in December 1920. The military leader of the rebels was Michael Collins who was very successful in organising the 'elimination' of suspected spies and secret policemen.

The British government had to choose between imposing martial law on the whole country, with all the consequent political and military implications, or striking a deal.

The settlement of 1921 gave Ireland dominion status, not independence by any means but one which recognised Ireland's right to seek independence. Ulster, however was already being treated as a separate political unit, having been given Home Rule in 1920.

Civil War

Immediately following the withdrawal of the British, Ireland became embroiled in a civil war over the terms of the 1921 treaty. One party which came to be called Fianna Fail refused to accept the treaty unless Ireland became a full republic and not merely given dominion status within the British Empire. The other party, which came to be called Fianna Gael, was prepared to accept the treaty as a stepping stone to full independence.

The issue that caused the civil war was not Partition which had already taken place without the 26 counties' agreement. Both groups in the newly independent Ireland felt that Northern Ireland would seek reunification once it became obvious it could not survive without southern cooperation. The question of swearing or not swearing allegiance to the Queen was the matter that divided the Republicans and drove them to slaughter each other with even more ferocity than that previously directed at the British.

The Irish Parliament, the Dáil, ratified the treaty but it was another two years of bloody fighting which divided small villages and even families before Ireland was able to get on with the business of building a nation. The divisions of those years have left a legacy, particularly in country areas, that is only now beginning to wither away.

After losing the war the Anti-Treaty Party under Eamon De Valera finally entered the Dáil despite having to swear an allegiance to the British Crown (De Valera said he kept his hands hovered above the bible and didn't actually touch it) and became the largest opposition party. By 1932 this party, Fianna Fail, was in power with De Valera as prime minister or *Taioseach*. He remained in power for 16 years and oversaw the creation of the present Irish state. The oath of allegiance was the first thing to go and was rapidly followed by a vicious trade war as Ireland refused to make payments on loans from the British, enabling Irish farmers to buy their land off their landlords – Britain retaliated by imposing import taxes and so on and so on.

The economic war lasted six years during which time De Valera formulated a vision of modern Ireland, a vision very much of his own perception. What is most important about these years is that the Irish had a blank slate and could create the type of state they wanted. Many of the men and women who had fought and given their lives for this moment had been socialists and feminists and people who wanted equality for all. What emerged was a lot less than that.

Over the following decades large numbers of Protestants left Ireland, women largely left the workplace and the political arena, censorship of literature became rife, education languished, and emigration became the norm – a terrible beauty was indeed born.

A BRIEF HISTORY

It is true that Irish history can become a little confusing. You may wonder why, for example, did William, a Protestant, receive the support of the Catholic states rather than James, a Catholic, during the Battle of the Boyne. Or why has it been so difficult for the Irish to unite as a nation, even when they have had a common cause and a strong leader. History often raises more questions than it answers and in a country like Ireland, which tends to merge history with mythology, this is certainly the case.

To go into the political alliances that were at play behind the scenes of the Battle of the Boyne or to try and analyse the psychology of Irish history is perhaps more than is required of anyone wishing to settle in Ireland. Historical events do, however, form a point of reference for a lot of what happens and is discussed in Ireland and the following brief history should help you to arrange Irish history more neatly in your own mind.

12,000–10,000 B.C.	Land bridges probably exist between Ireland and Europe.
8,000 B.C.	People first settle in Ireland.
4,000 B.C.	The first farmers.
2,500 B.C.	Bronze Age.
300 B.C.	The first Iron Age people – the *Celts* – settle in Ireland.
A.D. 200	Ireland divided into five provinces and ruled by a hundred or more Gaelic chieftains who were constantly at war with one another for land and power.
A.D. 300–500	Advent of Christianity.
A.D. 700–800	Europe in Dark Ages. Ireland at this time is a centre of culture and learning.
A.D. 800	Viking invasions and settlements.
A.D. 1014	Gaelic forces, led by Brian Boru fight off Viking invasion force at Clontarf.
A.D. 1169	Anglo-Normans, encouraged by Henry II of England, invade in search of land and power.
12th–16th-centuries	Anglo-Normans become assimilated, create walled cities and intermarry.
1532	Henry VIII breaks with Rome and uses the opportunity to destroy Irish monasteries and seize their wealth.
1541	Puppet Irish parliament declares Henry King of Ireland.

17th-century

Various rebellions lead to the *Plantation* , in which Protestant settlers loyal to the English crown were brought in to Ireland and given land. Gaelic lords were thrown off the land, particularly in Ulster.

1650s

Further attempts to drive out the English are met with massacres by the forces of Oliver Cromwell, the 'Protector' of England.

1685

James II, a Catholic, ascends the British throne. Talk of rebellion and restoration of Catholic lands.

1689–1690

William of Orange (Protestant and declared King of Britain) fights it out in Ireland with James II, now deposed king of England. James loses, Treaty of Limerick puts an end for a long time to talk of Irish independence.

1690–1715

The Penal Laws.

18th-century

Catholics hold less than 15% of the land in Ireland. A new independence movement, led by Wolfe Tone, a protestant, sought the help of the French but was defeated in 1796.

1801

Act of Union links Ireland and Britain even more strongly. A Catholic landowners emancipation movement begins, led by Daniel O'Connell.

1845–1849

The Famine.

1880s

The Land League begins to demand reduced rents and better tenure for Catholic farmers.

1879–1882	The Land War.
1892	Gladstone re-elected prime minister in England. Ulster Unionists, now an organised and coherent group, prepare to fight to stay in the Union. Home Rule Bill thrown out by House of Lords.
1912	Home Rule for Ireland bill passed. Suspended by the outbreak of war in 1914 before it can be implemented.
1916	The Easter Rising
1918	Republican parliamentarians elected to the British Parliament but they refuse to go, forming instead the Irish Parliament and declaring Irish Independence.
1919–1921	Anglo Irish War. Ireland divided into six northern counties and twenty six southern counties.
1921	Irish Civil War.
1921–1968	Northern Ireland remains a divided sectarian but relatively peaceful state.
1968	Civil rights protests begin.
1972	Bloody Sunday. Fourteen Catholic civilians are killed by the British army.
1970–1993	IRA campaigns of terror aimed at the British army and mainland civilian targets. Various attempts at power sharing fail. Genuine improvements made in the housing and job prospects of Catholics.

1993   Gerry Adams and John Hume meet to agree on a blueprint for a ceasefire.

1994   The IRA declare a permanent ceasefire, followed by protestant paramilitary organisations.

1995   Gerry Adams meets and holds talks with President Clinton in the United States. Direct discussions between the IRA and the British look likely. The IRA states that its goals are the complete removal of all weapons from Northern Ireland. British troops begin a staged withdrawal.

Chapter Three

A LOAD OF OLD BLARNEY

In the bolder species of composition it is distinguished by a freedom of expression, a sublime dignity, and rapid energy, which it is scarcely possible for any translation fully to convey .... One compound epithet must often be translated by two lines of English verse, and, on such occasions, much of the beauty is necessarily lost; the force and effect of the thoughts being weakened by too slow an introduction on the mind; just as that light which dazzles, when flashing swiftly on the eye, will be gazed at with indifference, if let in by degrees.

—Charlotte Brooke, *Reliques of Irish Poetry*

LANGUAGE

And so we come to perhaps the biggest Irish myth of all – the gift of the gab. Somehow, over the years the Irish have been credited with the ability to sweet talk their way out of situations, to confuse the issue, to be silver tongued and naturally poetic.

To people who make a study of language, it is much more than just a set of symbols used to communicate and in many ways Ireland's relationship with the language exemplifies this. It is different to those of other English speaking countries, including those that experienced British colonialism and the language of the Irish offers a unique insight into Irish culture and an opportunity to experience much of what makes up the essence of Ireland.

The Craic

Craic, or its English form 'crack,' is a very important concept in Irish life. It colours much of what people say. Seeing the funny side of things and bringing a humorous perspective into chat is the basis of all good conversation in Ireland and the Irish ability to find humour in most things is legendary. A good Irish joke can reveal self-mockery in a far more perceptive way than the racist jokes that characterise English humour on the subject. In the west of Ireland the weather is very important both to farmers and to the people who live in the countryside. Occasionally in the summer a long spell of dry weather accompanies a north wind. This can even lead to drought conditions. It was customary at times like this for farmers to ask the priest to intervene and pray for rain. One day Father Riordan was asked by one of his parishioners to do just that.

'It's no good praying for rain right now Michael,' he told the farmer. 'The wind's in the north.'

Dave Allen, an Irish comedian who was very popular in Britain, has his favourite Irish joke which reveals a delight in puns that is characteristic of much Irish humour. In an interview for a construction job an Irishman was asked the question 'What's the difference between a joist and a girder?' His answer was 'Joyce wrote *Ulysses* and Goethe wrote *Faust.*'

Crack is the motivating force behind an ancient Irish tradition commonly known as slagging. This is an activity with quite specific but unspoken rules in which, in the company of good friends, one person is picked on and teased about some aspect of themselves, perhaps their clothes or lifestyle. The aim is to be as insulting as possible without actually giving the victim cause to be offended. The victim for his part must respond to the slagging by slagging back or somehow turning the joke against the attacker. The loser is the person who loses their temper or displays hurt feelings first. Losing your temper is very bad manners in Ireland and sometimes great fun is had out of making someone lose theirs.

In Irish politics slagging often gets quite out of hand when one party decides to break the rules and accuse the other of sexism or slander. When a politician goes too far it often gives newspapers a field day of slagging. In December 1993 the unfortunate Taioseach, Albert Reynolds, in exasperation at being heckled in the Dáil by a woman Teach Dáil said it was just like a woman not to let him answer a question. Needless to say the newspapers (and the other Teach Dáils) thought it was great crack for days afterwards to refer to his remarks and even more fun was had when he refused to apologise to women in general on the grounds that his words had been taken out of context. The same person's past career as a promoter of country and western music has had him labelled 'The Rhinestone Taioseach' – even better crack.

There's No Yes and No

One of the most significant things about Irish English is the relative absence of these two words. If at all possible the Irish avoid using them. This might seem a difficult task with such significant words as these but in fact most people don't notice their absence. You might for example, ask a shopkeeper if she has any cooking apples. A British greengrocer might answer with the price per pound, or at least begin with an affirmative 'yes, love.' But the Irish answer might take the form of 'We have, so,' followed by a story about them or an enquiry as to how you intend to use them. If there aren't any, you'll get a fine story about why they aren't about this year, which may well lead on to a chat about the weather this season, how difficult it is to get the supplies you need or any one of a thousand other vaguely related items. A plain affirmative would offend any ordinary Irish person by giving the impression that the shopkeeper isn't interested in any further chat. A plain negative 'no' would be very bad manners.

If the linguists are right then this isn't just a habit, it's an indicator of a way of life. The purpose of going into a shop, particularly in a rural area of Ireland, is as much to engage in chat as to buy the things you need. In a society structured in this way, simple polarities are unwelcome to say the least. What chat can you get out of a yes or a no? In the cities perhaps, things are a little faster and there is less time for the important things in life but old habits die hard.

Truth, Lies and Embroidery

A traditional party game among children is the game, called in England, Chinese Whispers. In the game, someone starts off with a sentence and whispers it to the next person who in turn passes the message on. When the last person gets the message they call it out and great fun is had by all as they examine the mutations of the message as it travelled around the group – so that it has become as foreign to its original form as Chinese is to English. This seems to me to be a very fitting analogy for certain aspects of Irish life, particularly, but not exclusively, in rural areas.

Everyone likes a good story and any newcomers to the area will find themselves being politely but ruthlessly questioned as to their origins, particularly any Irish connection, income, intentions, occupation and family background. It's a poor publican or shopkeeper in any village who can't supply the locals with a biography of any new neighbours or even passing strangers. Add to this the rather odd nature of some of the people who settle in rural or even not so rural Ireland and the scope for the 'Chinese Whisper Syndrome' is endless.

One person I know has been, over the years; a CIA agent, a drug baron, a hippy, a world traveller and many other things. His dress, hair, body-weight and income are all legitimate topics for public debate and the less he reveals to people the more the speculation grows. One elderly lady recently told how for years after her arrival in the area in the 1960s her neighbours speculated about her involvement in the sensational Great Train Robbery (a daring robbery that netted millions of pounds that were never recovered). When that story became obviously unlikely the proceeding ones were even better; first that she had murdered her husband and then that she was an undercover agent for the IRA. The story of that particular lady grew to the point where her house was searched under a warrant. A group of fairly eccentric but totally harmless new-age hippies, living locally for a while, became witches, who sacrificed goats until they moved on and were promptly forgotten.

Passing the time of day in Kinsale. Talk is serious business on the streets of Ireland and has a unique Irish style.

Such anecdotes are not examples of wilful viciousness or gossip spreading. They are not evidence of simple mindedness on the part of the people who generate the stories. They are a part of the Irish myth building process, part of the sense of an essential history. Each person in a small town carries with them a long unwritten history going back several generations at least and one that many people know. A new person seems incomplete until some of their story is known and they have become a part of the oral tradition which helps form the historical identity of a region.

BASIC VOCABULARY

Some Terms You Should Know

Irish English is not so very different from other forms but there are a few words and phrases which can cause some confusion.

A cup of tea in your hand – The expression will be used by a friend who would like you to stop and have a cup of tea and a chat but realises that you're an important and busy person who has lots of other things to do. It suggests that you'll just slurp down the tea without stopping to sit down or rest. Of course if you agree you wouldn't do that at all but it would be OK to stop for a short while rather than an hour or more.

A soft day – This is a description of the weather. It is the kind of weather which often occurs in Ireland and rarely happens anywhere else. It indicates a degree of raininess somewhere between mist and rain where the rain seems to drift around in the air rather than actually fall down but is too heavy and wet to be classified as fog or mist.

Below – Somewhere north of the speaker. As in 'I was below in the village today.'

Blow-in – Someone who has moved into an area but has no roots there and is just as likely to go away again.

Bowsie – Someone who is always getting in a fight.

Chancer – A person who pushes his or her luck, takes risks or deliberately breaks a minor law.

Chipper – A shop selling burgers and fish and chips (french fries).

Chiseller – A youngster.

Compass points – (east, west etc.) In some parts of the country these are used in everyday speech to indicate where an object is. Someone may live west of you or the salt cellar might be positioned at the north end of the table. It is best to have a fairly clear idea of the points of the compass at all times. You might also come across someone called, for example, Gerard Mahony West, meaning the Gerard Mahony who lives west of the village rather than the one who lives north.

Crack – This is not to be confused with the highly addictive narcotic. Crack means a good laugh and can be got without the use of drugs although alcohol is usually present at most crack getting sessions.

Culchie – A country person. It is a condescending term suggesting that the person is simple and doesn't know much about city ways.

Eejit – A fool.

Evening – Any time from about 2 pm to about 6 pm.

Feck – This word means 'I really want to say that other four-lettered word that begins with *F* but I'm too polite.' It is used in much the same way as the more common version only perhaps slightly more often than an American or an English person would use it. Often it seems to be a mark of punctuation rather than a way of expressing offensiveness.

Gaelic – Gaelic football, a version of rugby football invented in the early years of this century by the Gaelic League.

Giving out – Talking in a loud strident way or telling someone off. This would only be done in very exceptional circumstances.

Good luck – Goodbye

Grind – Private tuition

Hippy – A term of insult. A foreigner who dresses strangely, has an unusual lifestyle, or has left wing politics is liable to be labelled a hippy. It derives from the 1960s phenomenon but the persons so designated could be quite bourgeois in their values.

Jackeen – A Dubliner.

Louser – A disreputable and mean person.

Now, so – Right then let's change the subject/ what can I do for you/ what's the next item of business/ you have my attention. It can also be used in other contexts. For example a shop assistant, giving you your goods might use it to mean 'that's that bit of business done.' In any case when you hear it the context will explain its meaning.

Over – England. You'd use it in a sentence; 'are you going over for your holidays this year?' A more formal version of it is 'over the water.' This does not mean France or any other place accessible by sea, just the United Kingdom.

Pishogues – A fairy or magical thing, rarely used nowadays.

Press – Any kind of cupboard from an airing cupboard (a hot press) to a wardrobe or the kitchen drawers.

Scoroichting – (pronounced 'screerting') Another fast disappearing word and activity. It used to mean what men did when they all got together at someone's house to gossip and discuss politics. The Irish word has been given the English suffix *-ing*.

Taig – A still very potent term of insult used in Northern Ireland, used by Protestants to denigrate Catholics.

The divil a much – I don't believe it or I hardly think that eventuality is a likely one. Rarely used but well worth it when it is.

There's good eating in that – That's good to eat.

Till – While or so that. Used in sentences such as 'lend me your paper till I read it' meaning can I borrow your newspaper to read.

Townland – A townland used to be an area which shared common grazing and everyone within a particular townland had the use of the common land. Nowadays much of the old common grazing land has been enclosed or built on generations ago but in the countryside, with no street or road names, the townland is the only way of indicating one's address. The postman might have six families all living in the one townland and must know which family lives at which house. This can be even more confusing when several cousins all have the same name and live in the same townland.

Well wear – You'll be lucky to hear this expression any more but it's still about. It is said to someone who has just bought something new like a pair of shoes or a car.

Will ya wisht – Please be quiet, stop fussing.

Yerrah – Indeed. It is used as a mark of exclamation as in 'yerrah, that's not it at all.' It has a variant 'arrah.'

Yoke – Anything technical, mechanical or modern. It roughly corresponds to the word 'gismo' in colloquial British English but has far more uses. A yoke can be anything from a screwdriver to a supercomputer and is usually used with a gentle degree of irony. It is also an Irish way of thumbing the nose to all those jokes in which Irish people feature as simple peasants.

Some Terms You Won't Need

Somewhere along the line certain phrases became associated with Irish people which they do not use. Best known as stage Irish they irritate most Irish people and are extremely embarrassing when used by visitors trying to blend with the locals. They probably stem from the efforts of playwrights and novelists of the early twentieth century who tried to capture the cadences of the Irish English spoken at the time and ended up providing a kind of lazy shorthand for American screenwriters. Use any of them at your peril. Even with the best of intentions you will certainly sound silly at best and patronising at worst, if you insist on using them.

Begorrah – Goodness me.
B'jaysus – Dear me, how shocking.
Top o' the morning to you – Hello.
To be sure, to be sure – That's right, I agree.

Acronyms

Unlikely as it seems the Irish are keen initialisers, more so than the English who seem to avoid initials as being too familiar. The following are some commonly used acronyms that you will encounter in everyday Irish life.

UCC – University College Cork (similarly **UCD** for University College Dublin and **UCG** for University College Galway and so on).

GUBU – 'Grotesque, unbelievable, bizarre and unprecedented.' The phrase was used by Charlie Haughey in 1982 when during his leadership the Attorney General was found to be unwittingly hiding a murderer in his apartment. In that year a whole series of accusations were made about Haughey and his goings on and the expression GUBU was coined by Connor Cruise O'Brien to describe Mr Haughey's doings.

AIB, ACC – Two of the major banks in Ireland: the Allied Irish Bank and the Agricultural Credit Corporation.

Tenses

Very few languages have common tense systems so that confusion often occurs when, say, French speakers learn English well enough to translate what they want to say but end up using the wrong idiom or the wrong tense. Visitors to Ireland from Asia might not notice that the Irish use tenses differently from most English users but confusions can arise.

One noticeable difference is that Irish people tend to use the present tense more than the English or Americans. So your new Irish acquaintance might ask you "How long are you here?" when they want to know how long it has been since you arrived in Ireland. To an English speaker this would sound peculiar and would be taken to mean how long do they intend staying. In general, confusions don't often occur but when they do can be difficult to clear up since your use of tenses may sound equally confusing to the Irish listener. The intended meaning is clearer when considered in the context of the discussion and when you become more used to the tone and inflections of the Irish voice.

GAELIC

At the time of the Norman Conquest a completely different language was spoken in Ireland. It derived from Celtic languages spoken across Europe during the Iron Age. It has root words in common with Welsh and other Celtic languages which can be traced back to a form known as Common Celtic. Old Irish is the most archaic Celtic language and as such is closest in structure to Common Celtic. It was largely unwritten but was the language of spoken poetry and stories handed down through traditions of bardic families.

Because Ireland never became a part of the Roman Empire its Celtic culture was preserved to a greater extent than that of Britain and it remained a remarkably resiliant and rich language. It is thought that the Anglo-Norman invasion may have helped promote efforts to standardise the language, as a reaction by the Irish against the

Gaelic fights for a place in Irish life but as this signpost shows, is barely holding its own. Metres, kilometres, Irish miles, English miles – you'll get there eventually.

invasion. Various English rulers tried to wipe it out, as part of a wider political attack on the Irish but despite this, Gaelic survived and flourished for centuries, right through the Statutes of Kilkenny and the Penal Laws. It didn't become a seriously threatened language until the turn of the century and as Gerry Adams has pointed out, the Protestant apprentice boys who shut the gates of Derry against the Jacobites were Gaelic speakers.

When at the turn of the century Gaelic once again became a written language, through the efforts of the Gaelic League, it was thriving in pockets throughout Ireland. In many cases these pockets of spoken

Irish were isolated and had evolved, as languages do, in different ways in each area. These different dialects made it difficult to restore Gaelic to a standard form. Dictionary writers had to choose the correct form of a word from seven or eight different versions and it was not uncommon for modern words, such as bicycle and telescope, to have many variants between the Gaelic speaking areas.

The Gaeltacht

The areas where Gaelic survived were rural. Ireland in the middle years of this century witnessed a massive emigration from rural areas to the cities and as people left they adopted the language of the cities – English. Nowadays Irish survives in areas known as the Gaeltacht, is taught as a compulsory subject in schools, arousing fierce debate at times over the usefulness of such a subject, and is heard at certain times on the two television stations and the radio stations.

Like many other things in Ireland the language has become a political issue. In the early years of the new independent Ireland it was government policy to impose the language on the people and in many ways the way they set about doing that assured the failure of the attempt. Irish was the compulsory language of the infant classes, all teachers were graded on their ability to speak the language and very traditional methods of teaching were employed, filling children's heads with information about verb conjugations and noun declensions – a sure way to kill any language.

While Irish was the passport to success in the civil service and other professional occupations it was rejected by the thousands of country children who had no such aspirations and the language never left the school buildings where it was associated with the often cruel practises of the classroom. It became a middle class language, rarely used except in speech-making and resented even by the people in the Gaeltacht who saw their living language being expropriated by civil servants who just used it to further their careers. In more modern times progressive teaching methods are slowly filtering into the classrooms and Irish is no longer a compulsory subject in the final set of examinations taken by pupils. It is, though, still taught in all schools as a compulsory subject and Irish classrooms are still filled with an odd mixture of apathetic students biding their time alongside desperately keen students who still need a qualification in the language to facilitate their academic or professional aspirations.

The Irish have a very ambivalent attitude to their language. Many people appreciate the importance of its survival but few are strongly motivated enough to engage in the study and effort that it takes to enable them to use it well. As long as it is not in use in the homes of any city people it has little chance to remain a living language and will be forever fixed in the minds of most people like a kind of medicine – good for you but leaving an unpleasant taste in the mouth.

In the North the use of Gaelic has always been a deeply divisive political issue. Irish was associated with Catholicism and Fenianism and was for many years seen as an indicator of enemies of the state. Until 1992 street signs in Irish were forbidden and there was no provision for teaching Irish in schools. There are now a few tiny independent schools in the North which have Irish as the language in which all teaching takes place and, on a hopeful note for the future, some of the children in those schools are Protestant.

In the Republic the post of Minister for the Gaeltacht was created in 1993 and a subsidised, all Gaelic, television station is envisaged. Despite this, in a 1993 opinion poll, 80% of parents polled thought that compulsory public exams in Gaelic were wrong.

What's in a Name?

If the national language is a sometimes contentious political issue then the names of people and things in Ireland on both sides of the border are even more fraught. When the Republic was first established it saw fit to name most of its institutions in Irish so that Ireland became Eire, the parliament became the Dáil, the upper house the Seanad, members of the parliament became Teach Dáil. This has continued in the naming of all public bodies. A list follows for newcomers, although the names quickly become commonplace once you have spent some time in Ireland.

Bord Failte – The Irish Tourist Board
Bord Gais – The Gas Board
Bord Na Mona – The Irish Peat Board
Garda Siorcana – Police
Oifig An Phoist – The Post Office
Radio Telefies Eirann (RTE) – The national television station
Taioseach – The Prime Minister. This word is not pronounced 'Tea Shock' as some so eloquently put it. In Irish English the *T* is softened to somewhere between 'th' and 't' and the last syllable is unstressed making it sound more like 'thi-shach.'
Tanaiste – The Deputy Prime Minister/Foreign Minister

Very few non-governmental organisations use Gaelic names and most of the public bodies in everyday use such as the Post Office, the Social Welfare Office and the Tax Office are known by their English forms.

THE NORTH BY ANY OTHER NAME ...
In the North names take on an even greater significance, even the term to be used for the whole area is in dispute. To the government of Britain the area is called Northern Ireland while to the people of the Republic the term most used is just 'The North,' as if to say that it doesn't need to be given a name since it is really a part of the same place. To others, particularly those who believe in a united Ireland, it is called the Six Counties, to distinguish it from any idea of it being a whole political unit while Northern unionists call it Ulster to give it a sense of historical unity. Of all the names given to the North this is the least accurate since the area traditionally known as Ulster also covers parts of the Republic.

In the same way, the city of Derry is known as Londonderry in Britain and among Northern Unionists but just plain Derry in the Republic and to Northern Republicans.

Gaelic has had an influence on the way that English is spoken in Ireland. We have already noticed the absence of yes and no, which is from the Gaelic. It is quite surprising that Gaelic should have this effect on Irish English because in large areas of the country there is no living memory of Gaelic being spoken. Neither is this effect in any way contrived in the way that some commonly heard Gaelic words are. It is more that the language embodies the values of the society and if a new language is imposed then the language has to fit in with the old ways of looking at the world.

One very obvious Gaelic influence is the use of the diminutive *'een.'* This is similar to the Spanish 'ito' or 'ita' which indicates that the object is cute, tiny, childlike or an object of affection. The ending is sometimes added to English words so a small boy or someone younger than you that you wish to address in an affectionate way would be a *boyeen* or you might be invited to have a *dropeen* more whiskey before you go for a *biteen* of dinner.

Most place names are Gaelic in origin. Derry means an oak wood in Gaelic and many towns begin with the Irish *'kil''* meaning church.

ACCENTS

In the early years of the current troubles over Northern Ireland, bomb scares were reported on British television accompanied by the information that a man with an Irish accent had given a warning. Outside of Ireland, Irish accents often elicit some kind of comment from the listener or some form of prejudice takes shape in the listener's mind. To some people in mainland Britain an Irish accent is an indicator of a whole range of prejudices from assuming that the person is stupid, to assuming that they are eager supporters of the IRA's campaign of violence. But it is in Ireland where one's accent can really be read for its full social significance.

Recognising and understanding the various accents of the regions and classes of Ireland is almost as complex as learning to appreciate fine wines but can be just as rewarding. Just listening for a while on the street in Dublin it is possible to hear the broad vowels of the native Dublin accent in the shouts of the street vendors. Listening to some of the more classily dressed ladies in the department stores the accent of the Dublin 4 area can be heard. This is the more refined and prestigious accent of Dublin. On television can be heard the accent of the Anglo-Irish in the voice of David Norris, the gay rights activist and senator. It is more English than the most plummy 'Sloane Ranger' could produce. Often associated with the politics of the region is the distinctive Northern Ireland accent. The fire and brimstone speeches of the demagogue Ian Paisley are some of the most dramatic examples of this accent. As you travel west and south the accent softens, the vowels lengthen, consonants disappear and the language becomes nearly incomprehensible to all but the Irish themselves.

Chapter Four

A NATION ONCE AGAIN?

Shooting is a popular sport in the countryside .... Unlike
many other countries, the outstanding characteristic of the
sport has been that it is not confined to any one class.

—Northern Ireland Tourist Board
New Statesman, August 29, 1969

THE POLITICS OF DIVISION

In political terms, although the modern Republic of Ireland is a very young nation, there is a mature institutional framework. The same cannot be said of the country's social development and anyone spending more than a short holiday on the island will soon come to realise that Ireland is quite unlike her European neighbours. The Irish themselves are often disarmingly honest about this. On returning from Asia in 1993 the seasoned traveller Dervla Murphy described the experience of being back in Ireland and feeling, "that I'd come from the Third World to some dotty Fourth World consisting only of Ireland."

There are certain key areas in Irish life that have to be addressed if the country is to evolve into a modern European state. Various laws, especially ones relating to the role of women in society, seem archaic when compared to the rest of Europe. Ireland's relationship with its established church is an area where change seems inevitable and, of course, until the issue of the North is settled, Ireland's evolution into a modern European state may never happen. Many Irish citizens in the Republic have little interest in the complexities of the Northern Ireland problem and seem to think that by ignoring the problem it might just go away. An often expressed wish in the Republic is that the North – the border of which lies just eighty miles north of Dublin – should be cut off from the rest of the island and set adrift to fight out its problems alone. This will never happen and, like other central issues, the North continues to bedevil the people of Ireland.

This chapter looks at some of the unresolved tensions that gnaw away at the Irish. They are not the sort of topics to lightly engage in a pub conversation for they often lie buried in the heart of the national psyche but understanding the issues will help to understand some of the social and political undercurrents at work in the country. Let us begin with the situation in Northern Ireland and then go on to the relationship between the church and the state and how it effects the Irish consciousness.

THE NORTH OF IRELAND
The Creation of the North

The Government of Ireland Act of 1920 created the political unit of Northern Ireland out of those counties where a majority of Protestant voters could be counted on for their loyalty to Britain. The Orange Order, named after William of Orange who had defeated James I in 1690 at the Battle of the Boyne, was pledged to defend the rights of the Protestants. The Act created a Northern Ireland Parliament, called Stormont, able to pass its own laws, subject to the laws of Britain, and gave the six counties representation at Westminster.

The Protestant power brokers had every intention of keeping this parliament Protestant despite the fact that the Catholic third of the population found themselves with a nationality that they didn't want. The passing of the Act was followed almost immediately by terrible sectarian violence in which whole families were killed because of their religion and reprisal followed reprisal. Catholic riots in the predominantly Catholic city of Derry were met by machine gun fire into the Catholic Bogside estate.

Soon after the government set up the 'B Special' police force aimed largely at quelling nationalist agitation. The Specials were a part time volunteer force made up entirely of Protestant men who were allowed to keep their weapons at home and were called out to deal with the increasing violence being caused by the IRA along the border with the Republic.

The Great Depression

While the rest of the world enjoyed the Roaring Twenties, Ulster experienced the beginnings of the decline of its linen industry. In the late 1920s unemployment stood at 19% and those who were long term unemployed lost their rights to any state help and had to turn to the nineteenth century Poor Laws to keep from starving. The Wall Street Crash precipitated huge decreases in the volume of trade all over Europe, and Northern Ireland with its small range of luxury export items was one of the hardest hit. For about 78,000 unemployed people and their families starvation began to seem a possibility.

In the early 1930s there were riots in Belfast in which religion was not an issue. Among the near starving working classes, sectarianism was the least of their problems and Catholic and Protestant stood side by side demanding food. Catholic crowds stormed police riot vans in rescue attempts on their Protestant fellow demonstrators. When the police opened fire in the Catholic Falls Road, Protestants from the Shankill Road went to their support. The riots claimed several lives, united the working population in a way that nothing has since and forced the administrators of the Poor Law to extend relief to the hungry.

But the Depression continued and by 1938 almost 30% of the workforce was out of work and this in a time when women did not qualify as unemployed. Rickets became observable in the urban poor, maternal mortality rose by one fifth and Belfast had the highest perinatal mortality rate in the British Isles, higher even than Dublin. Over half of all deaths in people under 15 were caused by infectious diseases like pneumonia, whooping cough, measles and tuberculosis. In Britain the comparable rate was about 25%.

The 1937 constitution in the Republic, by laying claim to sovereignty of the North and declaring the special position of the Catholic Church within the government of the state, ensured that relations between Catholics and Protestants did not improve. The constitution was ratified by a marginal majority and gave Protestant leaders the justification that they needed for their own sectarian state. Northern Catholics felt abandoned by the creation of a southern state which effectively made sure there would never be any reconciliation between them. De Valera, the creator of the 1937 constitution, himself admitted in 1938 that unification would be most unwelcome since absorbing the huge numbers of unemployed into the fragile southern economy would probably destroy it.

World War II

Worse was to come. The Second World War hit what remaining shipbuilding yards Belfast still had and night after night the homes of those barely fit to survive in normal conditions were bombed by German planes. The Republic remained neutral during the war and enemy planes were able to use the lights of Dublin to help pinpoint Belfast. As recently as 1993 the Protestant leader Ian Paisley used this as a reason for not entering into negotiations with the government of the south who, he said, could not be trusted. In 1940 the British began to consider bargaining unification in return for the use of Irish ports and entry into the war on the part of Eire, as the Republic was then called. De Valera refused and his later ill-judged condolences with the German people at Hitler's death only served to widen the gap between the Catholic people of the North, many of whom had lost homes and relatives in German air raids, and the Republic.

The North had provided a vital strategic base for the Allies and in the postwar economic boom it had been promised all the benefits of the new welfare state. By 1948 an agreement was signed which gave the North of Ireland equality with Britain as regards pensions, unemployment pay, family allowances, free health care and sickness benefits. Overnight this made an enormous improvement in the lives of the working classes of the North and set an even larger wedge between the Catholics of the North and the Republic. Unification at this stage would render everyone in the North far worse off.

One effect of the new socialist changes taking place in Britain further divided the people of Northern Ireland. By extending the British provision of free state education to Northern Ireland the government unwittingly created a sectarian education system in the North. The 1944 Education Act provided for religious education in the schools but the Catholic Church in the North saw that provision as being for the Protestant religion, undermining their power to educate Catholic children. Consequent wrangling led to delays in implementing any reform at all and made sure that Catholic and

Protestant children never came into contact throughout their education, nowadays lasting well into their late teens. In 1992 I talked to some Catholic boys in Cookstown, a small town in County Armagh, who had no contact at all with their Protestant peers and knew of only one Catholic child who attended a state school because his parents wanted him to get the benefit of the superior educational resources.

Postwar Reconstruction

The two issues directly responsible for the 'Troubles' (a commonly used euphemism for the political violence in the North) were housing and employment and came as a side effect of the reforms taking place in Britain in those early postwar years. During the war the Luftwaffe did more damage in Belfast and Derry than in any British city and vast tracts of substandard housing were destroyed or left uninhabitable.

Rebuilding was slow and allocation of houses was sectarian and discriminatory. For example, in 1967 in Dungannon, a town equally divided between Catholics and Protestants, 34 Catholic families had been given new council houses as opposed to 264 Protestant families. Similarly in many different areas of employment in the same town in that year, Catholics were far less likely to find work than Protestants. A survey of employment in similar jobs taken in 1993 revealed a similar preponderance of Protestants. Local electoral boundaries were jury-rigged so that Protestants dominated local councils where housing and public employment were determined. Only ratepayers could vote in local elections, so by denying Catholics housing they could be prevented from voting for their own representatives. In Derry, two thirds of the population were Catholic yet the local council was still dominated by Protestants. In local government jobs Catholics were equally represented as a whole but closer inspection showed that the majority were employed at the lower levels.

By the late 1960s there were numerous organisations becoming increasingly strident in their support of democracy and equal rights for the people of Northern Ireland.

A sign at the side of the road in the peaceful countryside of County Armagh indicates the loyalties of the people.

The Troubles

In light of the grave and openly admitted discrimination against Catholics which characterised the postwar years, the fact that it took twenty years to come to breaking point is the only surprising feature of the events of the late 1960s. The civil rights movement was gaining a voice first as a peaceful pressure group and in a short while, as more and more young people became involved, as active demonstrators. The IRA at this time had little support, was poorly organised and had very few weapons. A civil rights march in Derry in 1968 was broken up by the Royal Ulster Constabulary (RUC), a completely Protestant police force, and in 1969 a march was organised from Derry to

Belfast. The police offered it little protection as it passed through strongly Protestant areas and many people were injured.

More marches and demonstrations followed with the police becoming openly involved in the violence against the demonstrators. Finally, in 1969, the Labour Government sent in British soldiers to establish some sort of order. These men were at first welcomed by the Catholic inhabitants of Derry and Belfast who were nightly suffering burned out homes and other attacks. This brief affair was quickly over as the Catholics began to see their estates full of soldiers who were soon identified with the oppressive sectarian government of the North.

Gradually the IRA became the only force willing and able to protect Catholic people in their homes. From stone throwing at the British, many of whom had little or no understanding of the issues involved, children graduated to the art of the petrol bomb. Soldiers, thinking they were on a peace keeping mission, saw their comrades killed and took sides themselves. In 1972 fourteen people died in Derry after the British army opened fire on a peaceful demonstration – a day which is now etched in the memories of the Irish people as 'Bloody Sunday.'

Men arrested as terrorists claimed the right to be political prisoners, and many of them died while on hunger strikes demanding this. Bobby Sands, one of the strikers, who received international media attention, died of hunger in prison and was elected to the British Parliament just before he died. Since those days a pretty steady war of attrition has continued, with innocents accidentally killed, reprisals, intransigence and political bluster on all sides.

In 1970 the British Home Secretary said that the best that could be hoped for in Ulster was a manageable level of violence. He came under severe attack for the statement but in reality that is what has happened. The average citizen of Belfast has ten times more chance of being killed in a car accident than in a bomb attack or gun battle. San Francisco in 1987 had eighteen violent deaths per hundred

*This memorial marks the place where in 1972
thirteen Catholic demonstrators were killed
during a violent exchange with British soldiers.
Another died later from injuries sustained on
what has become known as 'Bloody Sunday.'*

thousand of the population whereas, in the same year, Northern
Ireland had five violent deaths per hundred thousand.

In 1993 something was happening for a while, with an increase in
violence accompanied by the revelation that secret communication
had been going on between the British government and the IRA.
Christmas 1993 saw the Downing Street Declaration, a joint statement by Dublin and London, that challenged the IRA to renounce
violence in return for a political voice in a new forum designed to
accommodate the different interests in the province. The Declaration,
however, only envisaged a united Ireland if and when the Protestants
agreed to change their nationality.

On October 13, 1994 the Combined Loyalist Military Command declared a ceasefire, following a similar declaration by the IRA the preceding August. Since that time the changes are coming thick and fast to the North. Talks between the major parties are noisily taking place and Gerry Adams is almost a respectable world figure, while the Unionist parties are clinging to their promise that the majority will decide the North's future. British troops are being withdrawn, checkpoints dismantled and investment prospects look good. Most significantly, nobody is being killed.

WHO'S WHO IN THE NORTH?

While the above account offers a background to the problem of the North it does not enlighten the reader about the various groups and individuals that dominate most discussions of the subject. Making sense of these groupings and individuals is a major difficulty for anyone trying to unravel the complexities and the following breakdown will be helpful.

The IRA, the Irish Republican Army, has had mixed fortunes since its creation in 1919. It became a powerful force in the late 1960s when it proved to be the only effective protection for many Catholic families during the Troubles. The IRA split in 1969 over its long term objectives. The Official IRA chose to relinquish the armed struggle and take up constitutional politics and has been inactive since 1972. Its remaining members formed the Workers Party, now renamed again in the south as the Democratic Left, led by Proinsias de Rossa.

The Provisional IRA is a wing of the IRA that emerged after the 1969 split and are often referred to as the *Provos*. At the time they differed from the Official IRA in that they were simply republican in philosophy while the Official wing had a Marxist viewpoint on the situation. This distinction no longer means much. The Provisionals define themselves in military terms; as an army engaged in a war against the

British military occupation of a part of Ireland. They have active units functioning in Britain and Europe as well as Northern Ireland and support units within the Republic. The IRA is militarily sophisticated and while they cannot hope for an outright victory it remains the case that the armed forces of the United Kingdom cannot destory the IRA. They have the support of a significant share of the nationalist community in the North and in sensitive areas like South Armagh, where there is a majority of Catholics, they have undeniably strong support from the local population.

Sinn Féin (Gaelic for 'Ourselves Alone') is the political wing of the IRA and subscribes to a socialist, republican programme of political and social reform. The party has little credibility in the south but much more popular support in the North. Sinn Féin was founded in 1900 in support of Irish independence. It split after the treaty of 1921 which created a divided Ireland and from it in the south the two modern constitutional parties emerged. In the 1980s Sinn Féin could call upon around 40% of the nationalist vote in the North. In the Republic and in Britain, Sinn Féin has been demonised by the media and politicians and the leader of the party, Gerry Adams, has often been presented as merely the political face of Irish terrorism. In reality, Sinn Féin has a coherent political and social programme that rejects sectarianism. The party is not so naive as to imagine there is a military solution to the North but it will not sever its links with the IRA as long as it sees a need for armed resistance. Agree on the need to demilitarise, argues Sinn Féin, plan for the removal of the British and face the need to persuade loyalist Protestants that their future lies in a united Ireland. Their goals seem to be coming about, although the game of political poker being played out at the moment may yet end in tears.

The UDA, the Ulster Defence Association, is a Protestant paramilitary group set up in 1971 during the early years of the Troubles. Despite its ideological appeal to working class Protestants it has been revealed as little more than a cover for extortion gangs. During the 1980s it was involved in many internecine wrangles and leading members were assassinated from within its own ranks. It is starkly sectarian in its nature and makes a point of murdering Catholics simply because they are not Protestant.

The UVF, the Ulster Volunteer Force, was formed in 1966 and openly claimed any Catholic as a legitimate target. It has gone beyond sectarianism, attracting psychopaths like the Shankill Butchers unit who during the mid-1970s committed more killings than any other mass murderers in British criminal history.

The UFF, the Ulster Freedom Fighters, is another Protestant paramilitary group closely linked with the UVF.

The SDLP, the Social Democratic and Labour Party, was formed in 1970 to represent middle class Catholic ideals and reject the use of violence for political ends. During the early years of the Troubles the SDLP supported civil disobedience and rent strikes. In the late 1980s it took votes from Sinn Féin and in 1993 its leader, John Hume, entered into talks with Sinn Féin in an attempt to end IRA violence.

The Ulster Unionist Party represents at the Westminster Parliament the Protestant majority in the six counties of Northern Ireland. At the time of writing, the Unionist Party hold considerable power since their parliamentary votes are needed to give a comfortable majority to the Conservative Party in Parliament. They are opposed to most of the ideas put forward for change in Northern Ireland.

The above groups are the main political and paramilitary groups in Northern Ireland and the following individuals are some of the more important faces behind the parties.

Gerry Adams is the president of Sinn Féin. He was a Member of Parliament for West Belfast at Westminster from 1983 to 1992. In the 1992 general election large numbers of Protestants in his constituency voted for the SDLP candidate in order to unseat Adams. He is a complex figure who cannot be reduced to the image of the terrorist so favoured by the British media. He has written a set of short stories based on his childhood and his book *The Politics of Irish Freedom* is a highly readable and coherent study of Northern Ireland.

John Hume, an early activist in the civil rights movement, became involved in the politics of the SDLP and emerged as its leader in 1978. In 1993 he carried out a series of talks with Gerry Adams. Their proposals for a solution have never been published but they precipitated the Downing Street Declaration of Christmas 1993.

Bernadette McAliskey, (nee Devlin) became involved in the civil rights movement in the late 1960s and early seventies She became the youngest ever Member of Parliament at Westminster and shocked the British public by giving a voice to the nationalist Catholics. She was attacked in her home in 1981 and shot several times. She survived the attack and continues to speak for the nationalist cause in Northern Ireland.

Ian Paisley first emerged as a fundamentalist minister in the Free Presbyterian Church that he founded in 1951. He became active in the National Union of Protestants whose sectarian policies included buying up Catholic property in marginal wards and refusing Catholics appointments to teaching posts in national schools. His pugnacious manner can be relied on to rally the impartial to the Catholic cause and the party he leads, the Democratic Unionist Party, makes the Official Unionists seem nonsectarian by comparison. He is known for his quoteworthiness and as such has figured prominently in the world media coverage of events in Northern Ireland.

ISSUES AFFECTING THE NORTH

A number of options exist in relation to the North's place in the future of Ireland. These three are the most likely to yield positive results and lead to a peaceful resolution.

A United Ireland. The only party which genuinely has this as its political aim is Sinn Féin. The constitution of Ireland lays claim to sovereignty over the six counties but there is very little interest in the south for such an ideal. The British Government and the Irish Government are committed to fulfilling the desires of the majority and for the foreseeable future the majority in the North is in favour of remaining a province of the United Kingdom.

Power Sharing. The possibility exists for a devolved state to be created in the six counties which would represent the interests of all of its citizens and which would allow both the governments of Britain and the Republic to have some kind of say in the running of the North's affairs. This seems to be the only possible way of dealing peacefully with the problem. Unionists, however, see this as the first step towards unification and while the Official Unionists pay lip service to the notion there is no real enthusiasm for the idea. One suspects that when Ian Paisley fiercely denounces power sharing as a Vatican plot designed to rob Protestants of their identity he is saying aloud what all hard-line Unionists think.

Making a deal with the IRA. Ceasefires and peace talks are only the first step on a long path to a solution but hopes are high that the parties are now travelling in the same direction. Either way a political solution now looks like the most likely outcome but just what form it will take and how lasting a solution it will be remains in the hands of the power brokers. The recent release of some IRA prisoners within Ireland has meant that the peace process continues to gather the momentum it needs to be successful.

The gable end of a demolished house is all that remains of the area known as Free Derry, a no go area for police and British troops during the 1970s.

A WORKING KNOWLEDGE

The newcomer trying to understand and follow developments in Northern Ireland needs to recognise the various acronyms, individuals and issues mentioned above. It also helps to have a nodding acquaintance with the following terms.

The Anglo-Irish Agreement of 1985 made history by allowing the Republic to contribute to policy making in Northern Ireland. It established an intergovernmental conference to discuss security and border cooperation. It pledged to make no political changes without the consent of the majority of people in Northern Ireland. It was opposed by all Unionist parties who withheld all support.

The Downing Street Declaration of 1993, signed by the British and Irish governments, was heralded as a new chapter in Anglo-Irish affairs, promising to end violence by inviting Sinn Féin to abandon the gun and enter political talks. Nationalists, however, remained suspicious of the document and without the support of Sinn Féin the Declaration will never get off the ground. In the Declaration, Britain admits for the first time that it has no economic, military or selfish motive in maintaining the union with Northern Ireland.

The Special Powers Act of 1922 was passed as a temporary measure but was still in use during the Troubles. It allowed the government to 'take such steps and issue all such orders as may be necessary for preserving the peace and maintaining order,' in other words, the government could do whatever they wanted. In 1973 it was supplemented by the Northern Ireland Emergency Provisions Act which did away with jury trials for those accused of terrorism, changed the rules governing evidence and allowed lengthy detention without charge. In 1974 the Prevention of Terrorism Act added more powers, allowing for the exclusion of individuals from the British mainland and the arrest of suspected terrorists without a warrant. It also extended the length of time for which a suspected terrorist could be detained without charges to a total of seven days.

Stormont is the name of a suburb of Belfast which holds the building in which the Parliament of Northern Ireland met before its dissolution in 1972. Its disappearance was felt at the time to be a Republican victory as it represented the power base of the Protestant community.

The Shankill Road is a street in the centre of Belfast running roughly east-west and set firmly within Protestant dominated housing estates. It has been the scene of countless riots and bomb attacks.

The Falls Road is the Catholic equivalent of the Shankill Road. It runs NE/SW through the city and is surrounded by Catholic housing estates. It too has been the scene of many of the headline hitting events of the last three decades.

Free Derry was an area of Derry City which, for a time during the 1970s, was a no-go area for police and the British army. The area has since been levelled and housing estates erected with wide roads and open spaces. The original gable end with the famous 'You Are Now Entering Free Derry' sign still stands. Nearby is the monument erected to the memory of those who died on Bloody Sunday.

THE CHURCH AND THE STATE

Closely and terribly linked with the issue of a united Ireland are the roles of the two major churches within the states that they dominate and particularly the role of the Catholic Church within the Republic of Ireland. Theobold Wolfe Tone, considered by many to be the father of Irish nationalism, declared that he wanted to unite "Protestant, Catholic and dissenter in the common name of Irishmen."

The 1922 Free State was a completely secular one, making no distinction between the religions of the island. The Irish people had the opportunity at that time to put into play the progressive ideas of the suffragists, socialists and liberals who had helped to make independence possible. But within a few years laws were being introduced which imposed one set of religious values on the whole population and by 1937 a constitution was in place, article 44 of which stated the special role of the Catholic Church within Irish society and law and which made some of the beliefs of its Protestant citizens, albeit a tiny minority, unconstitutional.

The 1937 constitution made divorce unconstitutional and banned the sale or import of contraceptives. All very well, you might say in a state that holds the Catholic faith as its guiding light and 93% of whose population is Catholic. But, what do these laws mean in relation to the further claim in the constitution that the Republic has the right of government over the whole island when the majority of the six counties are Protestant? As W. B. Yeats pointed out in the 1923 Dáil debate over divorce, these laws virtually guaranteed that there could be no reconciliation between the North and the Republic.

The Power of the Church

Having established the Catholic state in 1937, assorted governments went on to further regulate the lives of their citizens in line with the Catholic faith, and by and large no-one objected, except a few Protestants who emigrated. But the most telling incident of all came in 1950 when a coalition government began to prepare legislation providing free health care for all women before, during, and after, childbirth and further free health care for all children. How could anyone, you might ask, possibly object to that? Well, the bishops did. Such provision, they said, would be an infringement of the civil rights

of the family. The state, they said, could supplement the care of the family over its pregnant and nursing wives and its small children but it could not take complete charge.

In reality the bishops saw that health care might become family planning care, with information about abortion or alternative views of chastity and marriage. In effect it might interfere with the Catholic Church's influence over the family and its children's education. Government ministers backed down over the proposed scheme, the Minister for Health had to resign and alternative legislation was passed making care available through a means test to the poor only.

Effectively, elected representatives were accepting the veto of the church over the law, as if the bishops formed a third chamber of the Dáil with the power of ultimate veto. This event which marked an acceptance of the special place of the Catholic Church within Irish society and the laws governing divorce and abortion served only to widen the gap between the North and the Republic. This in turn gave the unionists ammunition in their claims to remain forever within the United Kingdom.

As the 1950s gave way to the sixties various groups were set up by more liberal minded governments whose aims were to look at the constitution in terms of the barriers it had set up against unification. They recommended divorce for Protestants, the removal of religious denominations from the constitution and removal of the claim of jurisdiction over the North. But the recommendations were never fully implemented. In 1972 in a poor turnout at the polls the population voted in favour of removing Article 44, the one which allocated a special role to the Catholic Church within the Irish state. But as many people pointed out at the time, without removing the prohibition on divorce the removal of the article meant nothing.

More than a decade later, after much debate and in the light of the huge number of marital breakdowns, a divorce referendum was held. All religious groups except the Catholic Church approved of the proposed change in the constitution and a referendum took place asking citizens to allow for divorce. The result was a negative one, endorsing the ban on divorce. This was not a only a moral issue but a legalistic one. Many people were afraid of the legal consequences. Who would own the marital home? Who would own the farm? Who would support abandoned wives after the husband remarried? In effect the people voted at that referendum to maintain a state where the values of the Catholic Church dominate.

Chapter Five

MOVING STATUES: RELIGION AND NATIONAL IDENTITY

There's no reason to bring religion into it. I think we ought to have as great a regard for religion as we can, so as to keep it out of as many things as possible.

—Sean O'Casey, *The Plough and The Stars*

THE STATE OF THE CHURCH

As we saw in the last chapter, religion has a special place in the life of the Irish, far more so than in other western countries. Its place in Irish life compares perhaps more closely with that of a country like Malaysia than with other Catholic countries such as Italy or Spain. The church and its weekly and yearly routines are the framework on which Irish daily life is built and for Irish people religion is both a pragmatic matter of seeing friends for a good gossip on Sundays and a deeply personal issue. Many Irish people have a particular saint whose life and sayings they study and to whom they pray for intercession with God.

But some recent figures suggest the changing nature of religious convictions in Ireland. While 80% of the people of the Republic attend church regularly, in Dublin's working class housing estates this figure drops to between 5% and 10% of the population. The reality of the situation seems to be that religion is most strong in rural areas and least significant in the inner city areas of Dublin, with a corresponding range of attitudes in the country towns and smaller cities. In a survey carried out by the Augustinian Order, the results were summarised as a general feeling that the church is distant, out of touch with reality, authoritarian rather than trusting and concerned with ritual and money. Yet the same survey discovered that the personal beliefs of individuals were strong, many of those questioned believing in a personal relationship with God, and in the value of personal prayer.

Pragmatic Worship

The daily business of religion can be seen all around you on your very first visit to the country. In the cities the churches look different to those in other countries since they have huge car parks around them to accommodate the Saturday and Sunday congregations. On Sunday mornings crowds making their way to and from the church are a common sight and the newcomer to the countryside should be warned

87

to expect traffic jams and delays where they least expect it. Another common sight is the groups of people who stand around outside the church door while the service is on, half because the building is full and half because just standing there is almost as good as, if not better than, being inside listening to the service and taking part.

A Celtic High Cross, carved with stories from the bible, stands outside a church. For the Celts who had no books and were largely unable to read Latin, this was the most effective method of spreading the religion.

In homes there will often be a little holy water font by the front door for people to bless themselves before they leave the house and older people's homes will have a portrait of the sacred heart of Jesus in the living room. Beside it will often be a small shrine with an electric light in the form of a cross. This is kept on all day. In older homes the shrine will be an oil lamp. Fresh flowers are put beside the shrine every few days. Even the most secular offices will have religious statues or other paraphernalia around, hospital rooms have crosses up on the walls above the beds and schools have any number of reminders of religion. Whole shops are dedicated to the sale of religious artifacts and books.

In the country, the outskirts of villages always have a small grotto dedicated to the Virgin Mary which is carefully tended with a small garden and offerings around the statue. Similarly there are many holy places all around the country, often springs, whose waters are thought to be curative.

Many country places are also areas of pilgrimage where the penitent carry out tasks at special times of the year. Croagh Patrick in County Mayo is the site of an annual pilgrimage which takes place in the last week in July. Thousands of people climb the 765 metre mountain, many of them barefoot, to honour the spot from which it is said St. Patrick expelled all the snakes from Ireland. Lough Derg in County Donegal is the site of an even more extreme pilgrimage which takes place regularly during the summer months and lasts three days during which time the pilgrims eat only one frugal meal a day and do not sleep. The stations of the cross, a ritual of walking around a marked out set of twelve points which narrate the story of the final events of Christ's life is carried out, again barefoot. 30,000 people a year make this pilgrimage.

In daily life the church is also ubiquitous. Turn on the television at midday or at six o'clock and you will be confronted by the Angelus, a minute or so of bell ringing accompanied by a holy picture and a thought for the day. The morning news is accompanied by the prayer for the day. Watch closely as people pass by a church and you will see many of them make the sign of the cross. Television chat shows regularly feature clerics expressing their opinions on all aspects of life, sitting happily beside a politician or pop star. Most schools have a complement of priests or nuns on the teaching staff and any family gathering you are invited to is likely to have the family religious as a guest of honour.

Holy Days

Similarly, the religious nature of the Christian year is far more in evidence in Ireland than in other western countries.

Christmas is nearly as commercial an enterprise in Ireland as in other places but your Christmas card is more likely to bear a portrait of the nativity than a cute robin and the day itself is a religious and family event, starting with midnight mass, if you can get into it.

Easter and Lent are taken quite seriously, particularly in the countryside where people do make the effort for Lent, not just to give up smoking or go on a much needed diet, but to give up some pleasure in remembrance of Christ's period of fasting. A few chocolate eggs can be found at Easter but definitely no bunnies or egg hunting. Again the significance of the celebration in Christian terms is more important than the holiday.

St. Patrick's Day may come as a major disappointment to any American visitor to the island expecting a New York style celebration. It is a quiet religious event, with parades put on half heartedly since the tourist season isn't really under way in March. The saint is known familiarly to all as just plain Patrick, or more familiarly as Paddy, the founder of the Christian Church in Ireland and his life story, including his grand snake act, is well known by the Irish people.

Other religious days are at least Catholic school holidays with a special mass said on those days and often individual towns or villages putting on a religious parade, with shop windows decorated with statues of the Virgin Mary or the particular saint. In some places it turns into a minor competition between shopkeepers as to who can show the most devotion to the saint with their window display.

But as mentioned, the nature of the Irish people's devotion is a very pragmatic one. Attendance at church is rarely questioned since often there are no other demands on people and besides, who'd want to miss the gossip session afterwards to look about to see who's put on weight, bought a new coat, going out with someone new or going through marital difficulties. Better still, who isn't going up to take Holy Communion, and why not!

Weddings and funerals also display this quite pragmatic approach to life, especially in the countryside. When someone dies in the country everybody enters into a highly ritualised set of events which are designed to bring comfort to the bereaved and set the death firmly within the daily life of the community.

A funeral is also a convincing example of Irish people's compassion for the unfortunate. Strangers to the family will attend a funeral out of genuine empathy for the grief of the occasion. Throughout the period of bereavement there is a heartfelt show of respect for the deceased and the family that can be very moving.

The body is brought down to the house or the church where a vigil is held by the family. The old Irish wakes are really a thing of the past. At the service the next day everyone turns out, whether they knew the person well or not. After the service, conducted by the priests and members of the family, the congregation stands about outside the church having a discreet look at everyone else and woe betide anyone who isn't there. It is this aspect of the event which seems to me to embody the pragmatism of Irish religion. Why attend the funeral of someone you barely know? In the cities this rarely happens nowadays but in the countryside failing to attend without a very good excuse could be a slight to the bereaved family and would be a source of gossip for many weeks.

Weddings are an altogether more secular affair in Ireland than they once were. Couples prepare for their Catholic wedding with talks with the local priest and most people still have a church service but from that point on the rest is pure fun.

A Religious in the Family

To have a son or daughter join the priesthood was for many years a great honour and also an enormous expense. A family which could afford the expense of the education could hold its head up in Irish society. For nuns or priests who were willing to train as missionaries the training was paid for by the church and many hundreds of Irish people have spent their lives in Africa or the Far East in tiny missions teaching and nursing the sick.

Images of the Madonna are everywhere. This copy of Michaelangelo's Pieta sits by the side of a single track road skirting the south coast of Bantry Bay.

In recent years the honour is still the same but alarmingly small numbers of young people want it. From a high point in the early twentieth century, numbers of men and women entering the religious orders has declined rapidly. Between 1979 and 1986 numbers dropped by 24% from 25,172 to 19,113. Three years later the total number of religious was 15,634. Only 557 or 3.6% of those were under the age of 30. While over 50% of the population is under thirty, 50% of the priesthood is over 50. Coupled with some of the recent scandals involving the priesthood this trend suggests that in the next decade the numbers of people taking religious vows will decline even further to the point where the communities of priests, monks and nuns will all but disappear completely. Still, when the family religious comes home from abroad it is a time for a family get together and to celebrate.

The Practical Prayer

An example of the pragmatic nature of Irish religion might prove useful here. On a flight bringing me to Ireland the plane, a 737 I think, was due to land at Cork Airport which has no automatic landing equipment. It was a misty rainy day and landing would have proved difficult. The alternatives were to circle around and wait for the rain to clear or to fly on to Shannon Airport where there was the necessary equipment. The information was blandly given in the typical pilot speech everyone has heard and we circled for half an hour. After a while the pilot came back on the intercom and repeated the information, adding at the end that passengers might like to occupy themselves saying a few Hail Marys in the hope that it might help the rain to clear. Most passengers barely noticed the facetious comment but I could see several obviously non-Irish people (including myself) wondering just how much of Irish flight technology depended on the Hail Mary and how much on technical acumen. Anyway, the Hail Marys must have done the trick since we landed about ten minutes later, quite safely and without incident.

The Magdalen Laundries

In the nineteenth century many women, often from quite wealthy families, chose to set up their own convents, often taking on teaching and nursing tasks and generally acting as social workers might nowadays. In the first instance many of the schools they set up were free to any girl who wished to attend but they found that in order to survive private fee paying schools were necessary.

The Magdalen laundries were established all over the country during the last century to care for and rehabilitate unmarried mothers. The women worked long hours in harsh conditions and often ran away, leaving their children behind. Many women entered the Magdalen institutions willingly, having no alternative, but others were committed to them by their families, in some cases girls who were not pregnant but were thought to be at risk were sent to the laundries. The laundries functioned well into the 1970s in some cases.

The bad press which the Magdalen laundries have had in recent years should be put into perspective. The women they took in for the most part had no alternative. Their families had rejected them, their children would have no rights and they had no prospects of ever finding work or living a decent life. The nuns were performing a service both to the women and to a society which preferred not to forgive illegitimate births. Set against the unhappiness of hundreds of Magdalen women are the thousands of Irish women who have been taught and nursed by nuns who have provided education and nursing where otherwise none might have existed.

Pishogues

The old holy places of Ireland are also a relic of the pre-Rome Catholicism which once dominated the island. Many of them can be traced back to an age which preceded Christianity in the country as can many other ancient traditions or pishogues. Social historians tell us that during the years following the Famine a change came over Irish Catholicism. Prior to the Famine a peculiarly Irish form of the religion existed, seen most obviously in the Irish calendar which calculated Easter at a different time to the rest of the Christian world.

The Skellig Lists. The difference in the calendar put Easter and consequently Lent some days later than in the rest of the Christian world. This led to a great bit of Irish crack called the Skellig Lists.

During Lent people were discouraged from marrying, so in the late nineteenth and early twentieth centuries many hurried marriages would take place on Shrove Tuesday. However using the Irish calendar, Lent was still a few days off and the folk belief developed that those who really needed to marry could go off to Skellig Michael, an island monastery off the coast of Kerry where the old calendar was still in operation, and get the monks to marry them. People in Kerry still tell tales of their great grandparents going off to Skellig Michael with a whole wedding party and several crates of beer and whisky but they are unlikely to be founded in very much truth. Out of this tradition developed the Skellig Lists drawn up each Lent by the local wags in which they match together unmarried men and women in extremely uncomplimentary terms, suggesting the reasons that they should marry one another. They might even be published in the local papers and regional museums still have some copies.

Puck Fair. This well known and now over exploited event takes place in Killorglin in County Kerry. Since it occurs right in the middle of the tourist season it is little more than an excuse nowadays to keep the pubs open permanently and rake in some much needed cash but its origins are ancient. Each year a wild goat from the surrounding hills is captured, decorated and stuck up on a pole in the middle of town where it becomes king of the three day festival. For three days everyone drinks themselves stupid and then those still standing let the goat down and chase it out of town. This coincides with an ancient harvest celebration of a pre-Christian deity.

Wren Boys. Another ritual whose origins are lost in the distant past is the tradition of wren boys. Now even the name is almost lost, since where I live in County Cork they are known as 'ran boys' and few people remember the original ritual. In it, young boys would capture and kill a wren and carry it from house to house as a means of ridding the house of the old year and inviting in the new one. Lots of banging and noise would accompany their arrival, to drive out unwelcome spirits. The celebration still takes place on St. Stephen's Day, December 26, and is happily carried out by gangs of young children, who nowadays dress up in Darth Vader or Ninja Turtle costumes and go around the houses banging saucepan lids asking for cash. A resourceful gang can pull in I£40 apiece if they spend the whole day at it.

Fairy Forts. There are many examples of pishogues in Ireland. One which is still believed in is the power of the many ancient ruins that lie about the countryside. The richer Celts lived in compounds surrounded by a stone and earth bank, sometimes five feet high, and the remains of theses forts are everywhere, often in extremely inconvenient places. They could easily have been levelled by farmers who still laboriously plough around them because they are believed to be places of magical power. Most people call them fairy forts and it was thought, in the days when the Irish believed in the supernatural, that the fairies lived there. They were dangerous places to be in at certain times of the year and there are historical records of women being put to death because they had been out late at night and it was thought that the fairies had bewitched them.

In modern times you are more likely to see some new-age community dancing about the fairy forts at Midsummer's Eve than any fairies.

Banshees and Bewitchery. Elderly neighbours of mine also tell stories of their youth when it was believed that you could bewitch your neighbour's fields by burying eggs or a cow's hoof in their potato plots. Country people laugh about the superstitions but one suspects that a tiny corner of their minds may still harbour a belief in the old ways. It was believed that a death would be accompanied by the sound of banshees howling and people still treat any loud unaccountable noises at night with a certain respect. Bonfires are still occasionally lit on St. John's Eve upwind of the potato fields – fungicide works well on potato blight but it's as well to be on the safe side.

Irish Wakes. The Irish wake was an important part of the tradition of Irish Catholicism which lasted well into the late twentieth century and most Irish people will tell lovingly of their grandfather's wake where the family and friends caroused all night long around the open coffin of the deceased. It was a kind of celebration of life. The practise has died out under the influence of modern Catholicism and perhaps in the light of the expense of keeping fifty or more people drinking all night!

MOVING STATUES

Pishogues, pragmatism in worship and modern Catholicism all came together in this odd story which took a small Irish village out of obscurity and into world headlines in 1985.

It was bad year in many ways for Ireland. The country was divided over the divorce referendum and a terrible story about murdered babies filled the newspapers. Ballinspittle is an unremarkable little Irish village, the usual two pubs and a few houses. But one night in 1985 a woman tidying the Marian grotto there thought she saw the statue weeping. The next night others came with her and they too thought that the statue wept. First the Irish national papers picked up the story and then international newspapers showed an interest. Crowds began to descend on the village and suddenly statues in other Marian grottoes were reported to be moving or weeping. This event happened at a time when all over Europe people claimed to be seeing visions of the Virgin Mary and many people in Ireland took it very seriously. Statues were reported moving in Waterford, Wicklow, and Limerick and coach parties were put together full of pilgrims hoping for a sign from the Holy Mother in those difficult times.

In the autumn of the same year, just as excitement over the moving statues was dying down, some girls in County Mayo thought they saw a vision of Mary in the cloud formations one evening. The Bishop of Killala wrote to the national newspapers explaining the phenomenon in terms of unusual weather conditions. No-one was convinced and the coach parties headed to Mayo rather than Ballinspittle.

The story seems to me to illustrate exactly the nature of popular Irish religion which is quite literal in its belief in the power of individual saints to intervene in daily life. The event also showed the very pragmatic nature of the Irish. The Moving Statues brought in revenue to local shopkeepers who no doubt did their best to keep the story going as long as they could. One Christian fundamentalist, however, was so displeased with the fuss over the visions that he or she smashed the statue in Ballinspittle, which has since been replaced.

A Marian grotto. Many villages have such grottoes which are always well maintained and are sometimes the site of a religious revelation.

The sightings were not confined to the summer of 1985. During the Black and Tan War in 1920 religious statues in a house in Templemore, County Tipperary, were said to bleed and a young man in the house was believed to be capable of healing the sick. More recently 1,500 people gathered in Inchigeela in County Cork after a young woman visionary declared that the Virgin Mary would appear to people. Several people claimed to have seen both the Virgin Mary and Christ and several cures were said to have taken place. The church strongly disapproved of the cults that claimed to have had these visions since the first sightings in 1985 saying that the visionaries' messages all seemed to be condemning society, whereas the message of Mary in the bible is one of hope and salvation.

RELIGION IN THE NORTH

Although Northern Ireland is technically a part of the United Kingdom, in many ways it is far more similar to the Republic and one of those ways is in religious conviction and worship, if not in the actual name they give their beliefs. Church attendance in the North among Protestants is almost as high as church attendance at Catholic churches in the Republic. The church has a similar role in society in the North and laws governing abortion and divorce are more liberal but not the same as in mainland Britain.

The main religions in the North besides Catholicism are the Church of Ireland, Presbyterianism and Methodism. Religion in the North is of course not just religion but is tied up with political affiliation so that most Catholics are republican in sympathy (but not all) and most Protestants are unionist in sympathy (again, not all). In most other western societies religion is a personal issue. In Northern Ireland it is part of a whole set of political factors. The Protestants of the North see themselves as a beleaguered and threatened group, much as they did in the seventeenth century when church and state meant the same thing and when control by the Irish meant control by Rome. Catholics, then and now, represent a threat to the state and to the Protestants's dominant role in society. In Britain where religion is little more than a set of personal beliefs and standards it has ceased to be anything to argue over, let alone kill anyone for, but in Northern Ireland it has merged with the struggle of a declining ruling class to maintain its privileges.

Ecumenism

It is easy for outsiders to look at the religious divisions of Ireland and realise that the only way to future peace is for the leaders of society, the church leaders, to show an ability to work together and find common ground. There is a strong ecumenical movement in Ireland, exemplified by the friendship between the Protestant and Catholic archbishops of Armagh, who regularly appear together on television.

Rome is at the moment going through an acknowledged fundamentalist phase which makes life difficult for everyone and the recent decision within the Church of England and the Church of Ireland to admit women to the priesthood has complicated matters even further.

Chapter Six

MONEY, SEX AND WOMEN

... a land whose countryside would be bright with cosy homesteads, whose fields and villages would be joyous with the sounds of industry, with the romping of sturdy children, the contests of athletic youths and the laughter of comely maidens, whose firesides would be forums for the wisdom of serene old age.

—Eamon De Valera
Politician and constitutional architect.

ATTITUDES TO MONEY

Perhaps one of the undeniable features of Irish life is the Irish attitude to money and wealth creation. Some aspects of this can be illuminated by considering the various Christian attitudes to personal salvation. Protestant religion as described by the sociologist Max Weber encapsulates the ethic of redemption through work. To the many Victorian entrepreneurs of Britain or the Protestant landowners who dominated wealth creation in Ireland, or the many dissenting groups that left the Old World to find a new life in America, hard work and sound investment were a sure way to spiritual salvation.

This is not so in Ireland, where there has always been a slightly different attitude to money. Today Ireland has emerged into the twentieth century where wealth creation is the only way a nation can survive at all and there are plenty of entrepreneurs in the country and many more who emigrated in search of wealth and found it. But still, wealth is frowned upon and a good career as a doctor or, in this litigious state, a lawyer is a better way to make a living. There are fewer risks involved. De Valera's vision of a pastoral land where simplicity and innocence were the norm also had little encouragement to wealth-making in it.

Charity

Woven into these attitudes to wealth creation lies the fact that the Irish as individuals give more money to charities per capita than any other western European nation. The state contributes to international peace-keeping through the United Nations but charities like Trocaire are a significant element of aid work in famine and war stricken countries. In the 1985 Live Aid appeal on behalf of Ethiopian famine victims, itself organised by an Irishman, Bob Geldof, Irish people donated I£9 million – more per capita than any other nation. Walk down any street on a Fair-day or during busy shopping times and there will be a band of dedicated teenagers exhorting you to give money to some charity or other and most people, to their credit, never tire of the incessant

Dig deep – the Irish have traditionally given generously to charities and the street-corner collector is a common sight, particularly in the cities of Ireland.

requests and give generously. An interesting corollary to this is the Catholic teaching that it is not a sin to steal if there is a real need and if the person from whom you steal has more than he or she needs. A man stealing food from the supermarket to feed his hungry children might be in trouble with the law but not necessarily with the church.

Begrudgery

Perhaps a result of Ireland's strong sense of historical injustice is a feeling of being second best, not quite as good when compared to what's going on in Britain or the United States. Reasons can be found in the country's economic history, not least being the fact that for generations talent has gone abroad in search of recognition.

Allied to this is the very real Irish sense of *begrudgery*. Succeeding in Britain or the United States – the two places writ large in the Irish consciousness – is fine as long as the person does not get too rich, famous, or otherwise successful. Then the feeling that they don't quite deserve all this comes into play and the Irish person who has achieved fame becomes an object of contempt.

This reluctance to dirty the hands with filthy lucre has become part of the peculiarly Irish phenomenon of begrudgery. This is a complex attitude complicated by the fact that everyone knows it is wrong, that those who risk all to make a lot of money are doing the country a service but still it exists. Begrudgers are people who are characterised as spending most of their time propping up a bar and criticising other people's efforts. These efforts might be those of the government to guide Ireland through its passage into the twenty-first century, the people who set up businesses or new enterprises or people who, by their own efforts, have made a lot of money.

Begrudgers not only begrudge anyone else's success but watch over the efforts of others to become successful hoping that they will fail. Pop groups which have become internationally famous such as U2 have described this feeling which is that they have got just too big for their boots and could do with taking down a peg or two. There is a kind of feeling abroad in Ireland that the Irish do everything wrong and that if something does go right it must be through cheating or luck rather than because of the efforts of the successful person. Begrudgers affect wealth and wealth creation by first of all hoping that the project or effort will fail, then waiting until the failure occurs and saying 'I told you so.' "The Late Late Show," a kind of national institution in Ireland, occasionally devotes an entire show to neutralising this attitude by featuring Irish people and their successful business ventures or inventions. Even more often the chat show format includes people who have made successful ventures talking about how they did it. Many of the shows in recent years have featured women entrepreneurs in a clear attempt to do away with both begrudgery and entrenched attitudes to women at the same time.

Not all Irish people are begrudgers but all classes and groups in Irish society produce them.

The Lotto

A state lottery of some kind has existed in Ireland for many years and is enormously popular both at home and in Britain. When it was called the Irish Sweepstake it was based on some of the big horse races in Britain and Ireland and a trip to Britain could be financed with a handful of lottery tickets which were illegal in Britain and had to be smuggled over. Somehow wealth is neither begrudged nor disapproved of if it is gained in this way. Perhaps that sense of accepting one's lot in life has something to do with it. Lottery winners do, however, have a tendency to keep their identity a secret and whenever there is a big win the media stake out the Lotto headquarters trying to spot the happy winner. The region that the ticket is won in is always given and shops which have sold the winning ticket display a little sign telling the public. Perhaps that makes it a lucky shop.

The Lotto costs I£1 per ticket and any number of tickets can be bought. The purchaser chooses six numbers from a total of 39 and their choice is registered. Every Wednesday and Saturday the Lotto is drawn on television and the nation is advised if there is a winner. The prize accumulates until it is won so the stakes can often be three million pounds if there have been no winners for a while. In addition there are lots of scratch cards which offer cash prizes or a draw for a place as a contestant in a game show called "Win Lose or Draw." On Saturdays this programme, financed by the Lotto, takes place. A superficial game show format allows the state to give away thousands to whoever wins a place on the show. The show is poor television but incredibly popular. Contestants are guaranteed I£5000 and can win cars or big cash prizes.

In 1993 a consortium of people tried out a completely legal scam of waiting till the jackpot was very high and buying up enough tickets to cover every possible combination of numbers on the Lotto. Since the lottery pays out for three or more correctly chosen numbers besides the big jackpot, even if they hadn't chosen the winning numbers the lesser payouts which are guaranteed added up to an

107

enormous profit. Unfortunately for the consortium they were discovered and were unable to make all the purchases of tickets that they needed. They still made a lot of money. The general attitude to the event was one of fairly good natured respect. Like other societies the Irish respect a good trick, especially when it is legal.

Luck Money

This is a phenomenon you may never encounter in Ireland unless you are dealing with an elderly person or are in the country. Where two people are negotiating a price, say for a horse, discussion may go on for some time about the qualities of the animal and how much the seller hates to part with it. When eventually the price is agreed and buyer and seller have shaken hands and possibly even exchanged the cash the buyer may well ask for some luck money. This means that the seller must give some money back to the buyer. It will often be done without asking since the refund brings good luck to both of them. Actually asking for the luck money is almost impertinent because the polite thing to do is give it without being asked.

If you are asked for some luck money you might want to round the sale down to the nearest round figure. If you are selling and really want to ingratiate yourself with the buyer you should always give a bit of money back or just knock off the odd bits of cash. This is often done even in big stores in Ireland, as if nit-picking over loose change harms your relationship and makes you seem mean.

Prices

In Ireland a peculiar condition exists regarding the price of things you want to buy. In the big shops of course, prices are written on items and computer bar codes read out the price, just like in most other countries. But go into any small village or negotiate a service with a local tradesman, or even buy a tin of paint in the middle of Cork City as I have done and prices take on an elastic quality depending on who you are. This is probably true of anywhere with favoured customers getting better bargains than complete strangers but in Ireland it takes on the nature of an art form. In the Far East for example, the objective of the seller is to get as much cash as he can without losing the sale. Not so in Ireland where quite a cavalier attitude exists over whether the sale is made or not and other factors become more important. What these factors are is not completely clear to me. I have been charged as much as I£2 difference for the same item in the same shop by different salespersons so perhaps the mood of the assistant that day is an influencing factor. Who knows? No-one will cheat you badly unless you are a total nitwit in which case you will have learnt a salutary lesson in the art of Irish trading.

Another factor which should be taken into account if you are travelling around Ireland is that the further away from the big towns one travels the more expensive things become. This is no doubt partly due to the cost of transport but it is also because in small towns there is little competition and a long way for customers to go if they don't like the shop's prices. So, before setting out on a long journey into the countryside, buy whatever you need. Something like a replacement lens cap or unusual film or a battery for your watch could involve a lot of searching and expense.

Currency

Ireland recently redesigned its currency to match its new European image and part of the new design shows a portrait of the writer James Joyce on the new ten-pound note. The engraving of Joyce shows the great writer grimacing at the bearer in a pathetic imitation of a smile. In fact there are no extant pictures of Joyce smiling and I think it is extremely unlikely that he would have smiled for a camera even if anyone asked him to. The artist who drew the picture had to try and imagine Joyce's face with a smile on it. A further irony is of course that Joyce's works were severely frowned on in Ireland until very recently and it was not until the 1970s that his work was finally generally accepted as art. As many people have pointed out he would have hated that stupid smile but would have found it great crack to be plastered all over one of the most widely used notes when he spent most of his life struggling to finance his work.

The five-pound note now bears the portrait of Sister Catherine McAuley, a sister of Mercy who during a cholera epidemic in 1832 set up a temporary hospital for victims in Dublin. She was a wealthy heiress who used her inheritance to buy a house in Dublin where she opened the first convent of the sisters of Mercy.

The currency of the Republic is not legal tender in Northern Ireland despite the fact that most of the coins are identical in size. Irish shopkeepers will happily accept low denomination British coins and even notes, as long as the exchange rate favours them. Northern Ireland issues its own notes, different ones of the same denomination issued by different banks and British notes are also accepted there.

Displays of Wealth

In the countryside, where no-one can move without all the neighbours knowing about it, evidence of wealth can provide hours of speculation about how the wealth was come by and whether the owner is spending it wisely. Anyone who spends money ostentatiously is considered a fool and it is more common for someone to dress and behave below their financial station than above it.

An exception to this rule of not displaying one's wealth is in relation to the church. In the bad old days the priest would call out the amount of money each family contributed to the collection plate and special seats in church were allotted to those who gave most generously. In modern times donations to the church are less grand with each person giving about one pound at the Sunday collection which goes to the upkeep of the parish. The priest himself, especially in a rural area, makes a good living out of his parishioners who contribute twice yearly at a special service called the Stations and who pay for a mass to be said for their deceased relatives on the anniversary of their death.

Taxes

Despite the high cost of running state industries and the welfare system, taxation in Ireland is relatively low. Farms are on the whole small and farmers are registered as self employed and many of them don't, on paper, come into even the lowest tax bracket. Many small farmers are even given a state subsidy in order to supplement their low incomes from milk. Much government income comes from indirect taxes such as sales tax and value added tax (VAT).

A complaint of the civil servants in Ireland is that they are the driving force in the economy since they are relatively highly paid and yet their spending power is curtailed by taxation. They pay both income tax and sales tax. The cities are also penalised by property tax as well as local rates while in the country many people don't pay any rates. In addition, all creative artists pay no tax which could explain why so many famous people live here, or at least say they do! Tax evasion is widespread in Ireland and in 1993 the government offered an amnesty to all tax dodgers to come clean and state all their income in exchange for freedom from prosecution.

SEXUAL MORES

The less said about some of the old attitudes towards sex and sexuality in Ireland the better. It is probably in this area that Irish thinking has undergone the most massive changes of all. Other chapters look at the way that unmarried mothers and illegitimate children were treated in the quite recent past but more to the point is what the interested new arrival to Ireland can expect from potential partners.

A recent survey undertaken among young Irish people showed some interesting attitudes to sex, possible partners and marriage. A large proportion of young people in Ireland, according to the survey, believe in what is currently known as serial monogamy – 80% of the sample tested having no more than two sexual partners so far. The age at which young Irish people engage in sexual activity varies a great

deal from early teenage years to the late twenties, with the majority experienced by their early twenties. Age of first sexual encounter varies with class, poorer teenagers tending to become experienced at a younger age. Marriage is in steep decline, Ireland having the lowest rate of marriage per capita in the European Union but the highest rate of fertility at 2.11 children per woman. Eighteen percent of all children are now born out of marriage and the idea of the need for chastity before marriage is low on 90% of young people's priorities and a similar number believing cohabitation without marriage was acceptable.

Within marriage, fidelity is high according to the survey, although large numbers of married people are separated with one spouse looking after the children. If promiscuity ever existed in Ireland the threat of AIDS and the need for safe sex has made the casual pick up a very unlikely event.

Reports of rape and attacks against women have increased every year since the 1970s. In 1991, 110 rapes and 245 assaults were reported to the Guards. That is a much lower figure than for other European countries and the increase may be due to increased willingness to report sexual assaults rather than more attacks.

ATTITUDES TO WOMEN

Male chauvinism is alive and well and living in rural Ireland. In order to understand that this is not just sour grapes or resentment on the part of a foreigner it is necessary to look again at that 1937 constitution that seems to have caused so many problems in the following years.

The constitution was written at a time when the vision of Ireland which opens the chapter was proposed by a leading politician. Implicit in it are women who preside over firesides rather than offices, classrooms or hospitals and men whose days are spent in manual labour. The place of women is set squarely in the home. When the constitution was written it specifically referred to the role of women in Irish society:

> In particular, the state recognises that by her life within the home, woman gives to the state a support without which the common good cannot be achieved.
> The state shall, therefore, endeavour to ensure that mothers shall not be obliged by economic necessity to engage in labour to the neglect of their duties in the home.

Labour which makes them neglect their duties in the home! The state cannot achieve common good it would seem unless women are in the home! The constitution of Ireland is not unique in embodying the principles of a forgotten age but it is always interesting to consider the framework around which a society has been built and in this case the tone was set, primarily by De Valera, at a time when the role of women in Irish society was accepted as at least passive and domestic, if not just plain subservient.

Of course despite this there are many very successful women in Ireland today who run homes and jobs and bring their special qualities of compassion and empathy to all they do. The prime example of this 'superwoman' is of course the president, of whom everyone in the country is inordinately proud.

Ireland also has a greater proportion of women in the parliament than Britain and despite many of its laws and religious mores the young women of Ireland are as much in charge of their bodies and their lives as young women anywhere. But scratch many an Irish man aged 40 plus and underneath you'll find a man who asks 'Is the boss in?' when he comes to install your telephone or mend the central heating. A recent example who for his own sake will remain anonymous is a publishing editor who, despite the fact that a book is jointly written by my husband and myself addresses all mail and queries to my husband despite the fact that he knows it is me that will answer the queries. Infuriating!

Since Ireland joined the European Community in the 1970s several working groups have been set up to investigate why women are under-represented in management and academia and laws have been passed making discrimination on the grounds of gender illegal. But the fact remains that women are in general paid less and do more unskilled and part time jobs than men and that women moving up through a career often encounter 'glass ceilings' – points beyond which it is difficult for them to move on. When in 1993 the popular chat show "The Late Late Show" devoted an entire session to some of the new women Teach Dáils, two questions they were asked by men in the audience were; how did they cope with a job and a home and why should they have well paid jobs when there were men out of work in the country. It will be a long time before those attitudes change and until they do, will Ireland ever really come of age as a nation?

Chapter Seven

IRISH ATTITUDES TO FOOD AND DRINK

I only take a drink on two occasions – when I'm thirsty and when I'm not.

—Brendan Behan

EATING IN IRELAND

I have lived in Ireland for three years, before that I visited it once or twice a year for a decade or so while spending most of my life in London or Singapore. I was used to being able to go to my local supermarket and buy convenience foods, frozen cakes, instant dinners and so on. Better still, in Singapore, to go out to any one of the countless food centres and be pleasantly confused over what type of cuisine to try. Returning briefly to London recently I found convenience food in quantities that simply seem wonderful to me in my little backwoods home in West Cork. Marvellous breads, every cuisine under the sun, any number of instant or pre-prepared vegetarian meals, low fat desserts, just waiting to be picked up. I wonder that anyone in Britain bothers to cook any more.

I mention the above because it is not the case in Ireland. The revolution in pre-prepared meals and the enormous range of cuisines available in restaurants in other countries has not made it to Ireland. The most exotic thing in my local supermarket freezer is pita bread and I once scoured Cork City looking for some fresh chillies. That's not to say that local dishes aren't, well, all right. Irish produce is fresh and amazingly unpolluted but it has a tendency to be, let us say, potato oriented. On the plus side, Irish meals never err on the side of scantiness. The biggest problem facing restaurants that venture into nouvelle cuisine is that people simply expect more on their plate. Never mind the aesthetics, bring on more spuds.

Spuds

Potatoes, or *perraters* as they are known locally, have a surprisingly short history in the long story of the Irish. Legend decrees that Sir Walter Raleigh brought potatoes back from America and planted them in his estate in the west of Cork from where they became widely accepted but if they did arrive in the seventeenth century it is most likely that they came by way of Europe. In the eighteenth century they were a luxury item made into a sweet pie and eaten by the gentry. The staple diet for the poor, and that was most people, was oats.

By the mid nineteenth century potatoes had found their true home. Potatoes need rich moist peaty soil and Ireland has more of that than it knows what to do with. In addition, apart from the need to earth them up a couple of times in spring, they require very little attention. This left the peasant population with the time it needed to grow the crops that paid the rent – wheat and barley.

Potato blight is a fungal disease of potatoes which begins on the leaves and quickly works its way down into the plants' stems and eventually the tubers. If it hits in a wet spring, even in these times of blight resistant crops and fungicidal sprays, it can wipe out a farmer's efforts in a matter of days.

Blight has a cyclical nature and there were small famines every few years leading up to the tragic one in 1847. The reason for the severity of this famine was that the population had grown considerably and because it hit the country for three seasons in succession. About a million people died and a million and a half emigrated changing the economy and social structure of the country forever. What didn't change though was the dependence on potatoes and even nowadays a meal without potatoes on the plate can be looked at askance, even in the most exclusive restaurants. The Chinese and Indian restaurants that do operate in Irish cities have found it impossible to function without offering chips as an accompaniment.

In the south of Ireland potatoes are generally a kind of yellowy grey and partly mashed, with the post fast-food addition of huge deep fried fingers from a place lovingly called 'the chipper' which is the equivalent of the English fish and chip shop. In city homes the spuds are generally peeled and simmered in water until tender but in the countryside they are still flung whole into a giant pot and cooked for ages ending up in a dish in the middle of the table speared and peeled on the spot by each member of the family. Holding a hot potato on the fork and peeling it with the knife so as not to drop bits all over the plate is an acquired skill. Those left over are thrown out or fed to the family pet. Baked whole potatoes are a modern trait as are roasted potatoes. In the North potato cakes and potato scones are still in existence but the tradition of home cooking is giving way to frozen waffles or hash browns. Potatoes with the mark of the spade, that is the potatoes that have been damaged in the digging, are left lying in the field for the crows to eat. To dish up damaged potatoes to a guest would be a terrible insult.

The most learned discussion that is likely to be heard on the subject of food among ordinary people in Ireland will be about the relative merits of different types of potatoes. One of the more expensive and popular types is Kerr's Pinks, which grow to a large size and retain their solidity after boiling. Others prefer Golden Wonder but those loyal to Kerr's Pinks will denigrate Golden Wonder for their alleged propensity to break up after a good boil.

The Full Irish Breakfast

If you have seen this sign in guest houses or cafes in Ireland and are too afraid to find out just what the full Irish breakfast might entail, wonder no more. Whoever invented the full Irish breakfast must have had in mind the idea of population control because anyone who eats a full Irish breakfast every day of their lives is unlikely to live a very long or healthy life.

Everything is cooked in the frying pan – bacon, eggs, sausages and black pudding which is, in case you have never experienced it, a large sausage made from blood and other items which is smoked salted and hung and then cut into slices and fried. It is served up with soda bread and butter and perhaps honey as well. This is really laden with calories and cholesterol but it can also taste quite wonderful. All this is usually preceded by a cereal and juice so you'll probably need to go back to bed for a rest after eating it. In Northern Ireland there is an even more awesome breakfast – the Ulster Fry – which adds white pudding to the black, plus fried bread and assorted other fried foods.

A more traditional breakfast would have been porridge – cracked or rolled oats boiled in salty water and served with milk and honey. Of course in cities nowadays every instant western cereal graces the breakfast table and Irish people are becoming just as conscious of healthy eating as anyone else.

The Midday Meal

If Ireland has responded to foreign tastes and ways anywhere it is in the midday meal and in the cities. Pub lunches include all sorts of continental dishes and even the occasional Middle Eastern or Mexican dish. Pizzas are a sad shadow of their Italian progenitors but are ubiquitous and lasagne, or at least a version of it, can be found just about anywhere in Ireland now. A midday meal in a pub or restaurant costs about I£5 and, apart from ethnic dishes, relies heavily on the spud. Even a toasted sandwich will be served up with potato salad. The further west and south one travels the more the spud will appear. Many people have a feeling that a meal really isn't proper unless it has meat and potatoes in it.

Among working people the midday meal is enjoyed outside or in a pub or restaurant with friends and the main meal of the day will be taken at home in the evening. However, in more traditional areas, the midday meal is called dinner and functions as the main meal of the day. It invariably consists of potatoes boiled in their skins and a piece of meat. If there is another vegetable it is likely to be a vegetable I know as swede but which is called suede turnip in Ireland. It is a large root vegetable which is boiled and mashed and ends up orange in colour. Like the potato it grows well in Ireland and sits in the soil until it is needed. The meat will be roasted or fried or boiled and is most likely some form of bacon or salted pork.

Herbs and spices are rare in simple country cooking although herb gardens were once an important part of the kitchen garden and old houses can still be found with their patches of tansy or feverfew or mint. These were used as much for dyeing and medicines as for flavouring foods. Sorrel was once a regular part of the Irish diet and older people tell stories of picking sheep's sorrel or hawthorn berries for snacks on the way to school. Since hawthorn berries contain a powerful stimulant this might have made lessons quite interesting in the good old days.

Tea and Supper

Tea takes place around four o'clock in Ireland and consists of strong tea with lots of milk and slices of bread and butter. If it is the beautiful Irish soda bread made with sour milk and baking soda as a leavening agent you are in for a treat but home cooking is a rarity these days and soda bread more often comes in a packet from the supermarket but is still excellent. Supper is a rarer meal and might be only bread and butter in poorer homes. For a special tea with visitors ham and cake appears. In the cities the evening meal is most likely the main one with the family all together for the first time that day. It is likely to be eaten watching television, and varies with social class in content and degree of formality. If you are invited to tea or dinner in Ireland it is as well to make sure you understand the right time and the meaning of the meal as you might turn up expecting three courses and get some soda bread and a slice of cake! Alternatively, if expecting a light repast you might be confronted by an enormous plate of potatoes, meat and vegetables followed by a pudding.

Some Traditional Irish Dishes

Soda bread is still very much part of the Irish diet but Irish stew really belongs alongside leprechauns and shillelaghs. It is stewed meat, usually beef or lamb cooked with onions, potatoes and the odd turnip or two. Herbs such as bay leaf or marjoram find their way into the dish. Then we have *barm brack*, a kind of cake, which was once used to finish off all the fruits of the summer and which I have seen in supermarkets around Halloween. *Colcannon* is alive and well in some parts of Ireland. It is made with mashed potato and cabbage which is fried in butter and milk with nutmeg added. Geese were once widely kept and eaten and were more often the Christmas dish than turkey which is more difficult to keep and has fewer other useful aspects. Geese are still a fairly common sight in the country although they are as likely to be kept as pets and burglar alarms than for the table.

The real, genuine Irish traditional meal is bacon and cabbage and it can taste delicious. There can be few houses in Ireland where this meal isn't served. The bacon is bought as a joint of meat and boiled forever and the cabbage is cooked in with it, also for a long time. The whole thing, cooking liquid and all, is served up with the potatoes and probably some turnip. Anyone over the age of forty and brought up in the country can probably remember the days when a pig was reared for slaughter. It was salted and packed into a chest where it stayed in the kitchen beside the table to be taken out a joint at a time and boiled.

Meat processing is a major industry in Ireland and that consists mostly of bacon processing. Irish bacon joints and rashers travel worldwide and have a special taste all their own. The Irish have a jargon reserved especially for bacon. Greenback means unsmoked bacon and the word rasher is used to mean slices of bacon as opposed to a joint. Asking for a pound of greenback rashers will be readily understood by anyone selling meat.

Other Irish Delicacies

Ireland has the potential to become a gourmet's dream holiday. Its traditional foods are excellent, though not inexpensive by European standards, and it also has some very special items that other countries really can't compete with.

Ireland has some of the most pure fresh water rivers in Europe and it's a river in Ireland that is used as the European standard of purity. In its waters live wild brown trout, salmon and sea trout. Rainbow trout are bred and put into the lakes for the many keen Irish fishermen to bring home to the table. In addition there is an amazing supply of fresh fish and shellfish and in recent years small industries have built up around farming some of them.

If you drive around Ireland's coastline you will see close in by the shore what look like lines of the rope used to mark out swimming pools for races. These are in fact mussel farms. Mussels live in shallow water where they cling on to rocks or anything else that happens to be handy. Industrious fishermen took up the idea of dangling ropes into the water and waiting a few months. At the end of the summer they pull up the ropes and lo and behold they are packed with mussels clinging on for dear life and just waiting to be thrown into a pot and cooked. Mussel-fairs are not uncommon in the west and southwest of Ireland, with free tastings of them on the street. They look evil but are excellent eating, especially as they are served up in some of the finer restaurants, in garlic or lemon.

Also available, though not yet exploited to the full, are scallops which live in the shallow sea around the coast and just need to be scooped up with a kind of rake suspended from a small boat. Oysters are another farmed shellfish but in recent months the industry has been hit by a disease which is slowly spreading around the coast and looks likely to more or less wipe out the oyster beds eventually. Galway has an oyster festival in September. Fish abound and John Dory, mackerel, haddock, and pollack can all be found. Strangely, even in the hard times of the 1930s eels, which are freshwater fish, would never be eaten and if one were caught accidentally it would be thrown down for the crows.

Irish Hospitality

'If you're Irish come into the parlour' goes the old song and Irish hospitality to strangers, especially if they can claim an Irish ancestor (and most people can) is well known. Step over an Irish threshold on a social visit and the kettle will go on, the biscuit tin will emerge and if it's evening and you're particularly welcome, the whiskey will be taken out. You will be offered at least a 'cup of tea in your hand' meaning a casual cup of tea rather than a more formal sitting down to a bread and butter type of cup of tea.

The tradition of keeping open house to visitors goes back to medieval times and one of the stories associated with Grace O'Malley, the pirate queen, is that when she called at the castle of Howth on her way back to her native Galway and was refused entry she took offence, kidnapped the heir to the estate and gave him back only on the understanding that the gate would always stand open and a spare place be laid at every meal. Brehon Law demanded that every village keep a guest house ready for passing travellers and that they be shown every hospitality.

Visiting was the social norm in Ireland right up until the advent of television in the 1960s and highlights in the social calendar would be a wake or some other family occasion. In the days when beer was too expensive tea and tobacco would be handed out and someone would have a song and someone else a poem learned by heart and the tin whistle and piano accordion would get taken out of the cupboard. The little girl of the family would be pressed into a modest display of Irish dancing and if there was space and liberal parents some set dancing might take place. This goes on far less now than it once did, people nowadays being more likely to meet in the pub than visit one another's houses. Inviting a friend or two round for dinner is definitely an alien custom adopted by city folk but the usual rules of bringing some wine or an additional dessert apply.

In the country, even nowadays, visiting workmen will be offered their dinner in the house they are working in. When all of the local farmers went to a neighbour to help bring in the hay or do the silage bales they were given their meals by the women of the house. They're just as likely to drive home for their dinners now or all go into the pub together for a pub lunch but when there were no cars and the neighbour might have walked over the mountain to lend a hand it was an essential piece of hospitality. You are most likely to come across this old Irish custom of bringing out food and tea for visitors at a wake or a celebration of the Stations, when it becomes the custom to do at least as well as the person whose house it was at last year.

125

Eating Out

This isn't as dire an activity as it was a few years ago. In fact scattered around Ireland there are many famous chefs each with their own place and a waiting list for reservations and, of course, a price list to match. People will travel fifty miles or more to visit one of these restaurants which lie off the beaten track and whose fame spreads by word of mouth. There are many more small places run by people whose first interest is living the quiet peaceful lifestyle of the far west of Ireland and who use their culinary skills as a means of supporting themselves.

Kinsale in County Cork is an interesting place as regards food. It is a tiny fishing village which has somehow become a gourmet centre with any number of very classy restaurants and a food festival each year.

For the most part, though, eating out at night in Ireland is an expensive business and most restaurants serve very standard steak and chips type meals, even the restaurants which serve foreign cuisines keep several western staples on the menu and alter the taste of their cuisine to suit the more bland Irish palate. Most restaurants pay lip-service to the vegetarian's needs and for a vegetarian to eat out a lot in Ireland they'd need to be very fond of vegetable lasagne.

The average price for a pub lunch or a meal at lunchtime is around I£5. At night the price can easily double and a three course meal at a fancy restaurant will be in the region of I£20 a head, excluding wine, although price and quality obviously vary, as they do anywhere.

DRINKING IN IRELAND
A Pub Culture

And so to the biggest Irish cliche of all – drink. Now, I've been as inebriated as a newt on many occasions and loved every minute of it, even if I did regret it the next day but there is a certain jovial attitude to drink and drunkenness abroad, especially in connection with Irish people which doesn't really paint the whole picture.

Have a drink while you get the groceries. Once the norm, these tiny grocery shops cum public houses are now a rarer sight.

Let's look at the positive aspects of the pub culture first. An evening spent in one of the many thousands of tiny Irish bars, especially in the summer, can be an evening to remember for many years to come. At its best, full of good music and lively chat, the pub is a relatively inexpensive and fun night out. Many pubs offer food at lunchtime and at night, live music, room for children to run around and not bother anyone and a place where people can forget the bothers of the day. If anything is keeping the strong tradition of music alive in Ireland it is the pub culture. In any one small town in the country in summer there will be at least a couple of groups of musicians playing per night. If you are really lucky you may stumble upon some genuine traditional singers or you might listen to some rebel songs sung with real venom around the border in counties Donegal or Armagh.

127

Most pubs are owned or rented by individuals and that dreadful plastic pub interior which you may be familiar with in other countries is unusual. Decoration is likely to be sparse with old farm implements or old posters on the walls, a dartboard, and in the winter wicked card games, which you will never learn the rules of. If you don't want a drink of alcohol you can get coffee or tea or a soft drink and in the summer you can wander out to the seats outside and people-watch. In the cities pubs are the hub of the social life with different pubs specialising in different types of music. Opening hours in the country are flexible to say the least and best crack of all is watching the place empty at midnight when someone rings up and warns that the *garda* are making one of their irregular patrols.

That's the best of Irish pub culture but not all pubs can boast this ambience. You can tell a bad pub within seconds of opening the door. Around the bar are about ten or so drooping men but no women. The television is on, making conversation impossible and all the faces are turned vacantly towards it as they make begrudging comments at the news bulletin. As each one reaches their liquid limit or the time they need to return to wherever they came from, they peel away from the bar and slouch out. When they have drunk a lot they might get into a fight, or the card game in the corner may turn into a yelling match about some incomprehensible rule in the game, or the publican's niece might arrive with a broken down set of speakers and do old Lennon-McCartney numbers on her Hammond organ.

Worse still is the culture that forgives people's indiscretions or bad manners, or worse still their brutality, on the grounds that they were drunk. Driving while drunk is of course illegal in Ireland but in an under-populated countryside with a limited police presence it can often go unnoticed. Driving under the influence of alcohol is still not regarded as a serious offence by most people. Unlike most countries these days, where such activity is seen as a criminal act, in Ireland there is a certain tolerance for the amicable drunk. The police also seem reluctant in Ireland, as they are in most countries, to intervene

GUINNESS..
GUINNESS..

in domestic disputes, many of which begin on a Saturday night after closing time at the local pub.

If you go into any pub at any time in Ireland and count the number of women, there are almost certain to be far fewer women than men. This is especially true of country pubs and it says something of the quality of family life in some homes that so many men spend their evenings in the pub while their wives are at home with the children.

Nevertheless the pub is the focus of social life in Ireland despite the fact that there are many temperance and church organisations which work to offset some of the worst effects of a drinking culture. There are vast numbers of pubs in Ireland, a small village of perhaps 200 souls having at least three, all of which make a decent living for their owners.

Pub Etiquette

Whether you approve of drinking or not it will be very difficult for the lover of Ireland to survive very long without going into a pub and there are certain rules of behaviour which apply in them. The major activity in local bars in Ireland during the off tourist season is to talk about the other people in the bar but it must be done with a certain degree of finesse. Another pub activity is to draw complete strangers into conversation in order to draw out everything about them. If this can be done while giving away nothing about yourself so much the better. If you are a stranger it is best to tell everyone as much as you can about yourself and then they won't feel obliged to make it up.

The politics of Northern Ireland is a topic that is rarely aired in a pub. Irish jokes can be laughed at if they are told to you by an Irish person but you should not tell them yourself and if you really feel you must, try changing the national character of the idiot in the joke to your own. Remarks and anecdotes about the corrupt nature of southern politicians are acceptable topics of conversation but don't go too far. Politicians should be called by their first name or a diminutive form, such as Charlie or Dessie, for example. Do not talk about religion or other emotive topics such as abortion.

Buying rounds of drinks is a complex affair and, as haphazard as it may seem, careful note is taken of how many you buy and whether you are paying your way. Rounds tend to be bought by men and this is invariably the case if married couples are together. With a younger group of people women expect, and are expected to, pay for a round in the usual manner. People remember that they owe somebody something for ages in Ireland and you may find yourself being bought a drink in May because you gave somebody a lift in December.

Christmas time is particularly important in buying other people drinks and you'll get a drink on the house in your local pub as thanks for your custom. In summer, returned locals stand drinks to show how well they've done over in England or the States and don't always need one bought in return. But don't, above all, buy more than you owe because then you are regarded as either showing off or stupid. Also getting yourself half a pint of Guinness when it's your round and asking for a double whiskey when it's somebody else's will not enamour you to your new friends. Don't make the mistake of thinking they're too drunk to realise what you're up to or whether you missed your round – they do notice. Above all don't get into a round buying group of twenty or more or you'll never get away. People will go on getting their round rather than be called mean even if it is well past closing time. Apart from that, drinking in Irish bars is grand fun.

Guinness

A chapter on attitudes to food and drink in Ireland cannot end without some mention of the one thing that everyone associates with Ireland. Guinness isn't just a beer it's a way of life, from its role in the nation's prosperity and history to its reputed healing powers – I kid you not. Guinness is regularly prescribed as a tonic and was and still is given in small quantities to children as a remedy for various complaints. It looks different from other beers with deep purply black liquid topped with a thick creamy froth. It takes quite a time to draw into the glass because of the frothy head and the bartender will draw a glass of beer and then rest it for a while for the froth to subside and then refill it. People send back glasses that are not completely full or where the head is too thick.

Guinness is consumed worldwide although readers should be assured that whatever the stuff they are drinking in their own country tastes like, drinking it in Ireland is a very different experience. Perhaps the closest taste to it can be obtained from the specially designed cans which are designed to give the draught Guinness taste. There are many foreign beers available in Ireland which are becoming very trendy among Dublin yuppies, however, few serious drinkers try anything other than Guinness or one of the other black beers brewed in Ireland. Much guff is talked about the state of the pumps and the distance from the barrel to the pump and the varying qualities of the brew in different pubs in Dublin. But most pubs do a roaring trade whatever the length of the pipes and sending a pint back because it doesn't meet one's gastronomic standards is likely to be met with a request to take your business somewhere else.

Some Irish drinkers may tell you that the more you drink the healthier you get but we warned, Irish stout is an acquired taste.

Whiskey

Irish whiskey is another very popular drink and has been brewed in Ireland for centuries. More recent additions are some liqueurs and mixtures such as Irish Mist or Baileys Irish Cream which are very rich sweet drinks. Poteen is illicitly brewed whiskey made probably in someone's back-yard and its quality varies with its source but it is still widely available and a bottle will cost around I£7. It is a white liquid similar in taste to gin rather than whiskey and is often drunk mixed with Guinness in what must be a potentially lethal cocktail.

Irish whiskey is not only spelt differently but also tastes different to Scotch and other whiskies. Both types are based on barley, part of which is malted and this accounts for one of the differences. Malt for Irish whiskey is dried in a closed kiln whereas Scotch uses an open peat fire and consequently has a smoky quality that is absent from the Irish drink. The other difference is that Irish whiskey is distilled three times, once more than other categories of the drink.

The most popular and readily available whiskey is Jameson, which dates back to 1780. The Bushmills distillery in the town of that name in County Antrim dates back to 1608 and is a famous drink that is worth savouring. Bushmills Malt is the only single malt brand of Irish whiskey.

Incidentally, the word whiskey is said to derive from the Irish words *uisce beatha* (isk-ke ba-ha) which over the centuries became mispronounced as whiskey.

Chapter Eight

THE IRISH AT WORK

The train was over half an hour behind its time and the
traveller complained to the guard of the train, and the
guard spoke to him bitterly. He said, "You must have a
very narrow heart that wouldn't go down to the town and
stand your friends a few drinks instead of bothering me to
get away."

—Jack B. Yeats, *Sligo*

THE IRISH WORK ETHIC

Just the title of this chapter could bring a smile to the face of an English comedian thinking about new material for his stage act. The English mythological Irishman, as described in the opening chapter, spends most of his time leaning on his shovel discussing the best way to continue digging his hole. The national character that emerges in the Irish joke, deeply embedded in the consciousness of English people, is shiftless, work shy, simple minded and incapable of doing anything unless it is a very simple activity and then it will be done in the silliest possible way.

How many Irishmen does it take to fit a light bulb? Answer: Four; one to hold the bulb and three to turn the ladder. Did you hear about the Irishman who fell out of the window? He was ironing the curtains! One Irishman to another Irishman (looking up at the sky): 'Is that the sun or the moon?' Second Irishman: 'I don't know I don't live round here.'

Many societies with an immigrant community develop these stereotypes in their culture. But why should this particular stereotype have stuck to Irish people? England has West Indian and Asian communities which are far more in evidence than the Irish. The Irish have been emigrating to Britain for centuries, taking badly paid manual work, often under terrible work conditions. During the Second World War thousands of Irish men went to Britain to fill the places of the men who went to war and much Irish labour went into the war effort.

After the Second World War many more came to Britain, living in poor housing and being ferried from one building site to the next, working with no insurance and paying no taxes, saving their employers a great deal of money in pay and benefits. Further back in history, the Irish came to Britain in the nineteenth century to work on the many building projects taking place then. *Navvy*, the word which now means a manual labourer, comes from the term 'navigators' which was used to describe the men who worked on building Britain's canal system, most of them Irish. Much of Britain's infrastructure was built by Irish hands and in view of this the comedian's jokes can at times wear a bit thin.

The kernel of truth that accounts for the slanderous stereotyping is that the Irish do have a more relaxed and humane attitude towards work. They work to live, not the other way around, and in doing so make a valuable contribution to European civilisation.

IRISH INDUSTRY
Agriculture

Ireland's single biggest export industry is agriculture and has been for many years. Over five million hectares of the Republic's nearly seven million is given up to agriculture. This does not include woodlands. In 1992 agricultural products formed 24% of Ireland's total exports. The industry is dominated by the beef and dairy sector. These figures alone paint a picture of a largely agrarian society but this is not strictly true, given the percentages of people who live and work in rural areas compared to the city dwellers.

The central lowlands of the country are the more modernised with fairly large farms producing beef cattle, while the southwest and west are the primary source of dairy cattle. The east and southeast areas of the country produce sugar beet, wheat, barley and potatoes. Around 162,000 people are employed in agriculture based industries with the typical farm being very small, usually around twenty hectares, and run by a single farmer, perhaps with the help of one son.

Since 1973 when Ireland joined the EEC – now called the European Union (EU) – Irish beef and dairy farming has had the support of price controls and intervention buying to maintain prices at a level which allows the small farmer to remain in business. In 1991 40% of Irish butter was bought up by the European Union along with 52% of beef and 49% of skimmed milk powder. These products are stored or sold outside of Europe in order to maintain artificially high prices in the European Union.

A small local fishing boat waits in the shelter of Dunmanus Bay for another day's work. In the background is the ruin of what was once a home for children orphaned by the Famine.

Recent reform of policies on subsidies and intervention buying means that the small farmer will be put under tremendous pressure and the probable pattern for the future suggests greater diversification into other products such as market gardening or raising other meat producing animals such as deer, or afforestation. This sounds like a sound economic idea. Why pay farmers to produce unwanted foods when they could instead produce more profitable products? What it probably means in the long term is that the whole nature of the west and south of Ireland will change with the small farms gradually disappearing. The farm land may be given over to trees or swallowed up into bigger, more profitable enterprises using more machinery. In effect an even greater depopulation of the countryside than is taking place already.

Forestry

A potential future source of employment and land use is forestry. From about 1% of total land under forest at the turn of the century European Union grants have encouraged that figure to rise to 7% by 1992, although this is tiny compared to the European Union average of 24%. Ireland has almost perfect conditions for trees – a wet climate and highly fertile soil make growth rates in Ireland far higher than in countries where forestry is a major industry. At the moment forestry work is undertaken by a semi-state industry called *Coilte*. It administers 400,000 hectares of land and plans to plant 23,000 hectares per year. Farmers can get subsidies of up to 85% of their costs for planting forests. That comes to about I£800 per hectare as well as grants for maintaining the forests. But old habits die hard and many people are reluctant to give up hard won fertile fields to forests which may not turn a profit for decades.

Food Processing

Also related to, and highly dependent on agriculture, is the food processing industry. Unlike many other industries in Ireland it is still Irish owned and a large portion of the profits stay in the country. It produces about 20% of Irish exports. It is dominated by the dairy produce sector which employs about 9,000 people. It suffers, however, from the same problem that other Irish industries face in that it is comparatively small in relation to the big European groups with which it is competing.

Tourism

One result of the changing nature of Irish agriculture has been the way that many Irish land owners have turned their attention to another industry altogether in their search to stay solvent. Tourism is a major growth industry in Ireland. It employs 8,700 people, albeit on a seasonal basis and contributes I£500 million to exports. Some three million people visit Ireland every year, mostly during the months of

June, July and August. The tourist industry generates all this employment and wealth under some exceptionally difficult conditions. Until very recently air fares to Ireland have been high, ferry journeys can be long and expensive, car hire is also relatively expensive, the tourist season is very short and there is the ongoing burden of the reputation for violence in Northern Ireland. The distinction between the north and south of Ireland is not always understood by people planning their holidays and even those who do appreciate the difference have tended to think that the whole of Northern Ireland is bristling with gunmen and bombs and riots. In reality, only a few inner city, working class areas and the southern part of County Armagh received an overwhelming proportion of the violence.

Until 1993 there was an added problem arising from the insistence that transatlantic flights had to stop at Shannon Airport. The airport, in the far west of the country, was built because transatlantic flights could not make the long haul from mainland Europe to the United States without refuelling. Without those stopovers the airport had little function so that when planes could eventually make the journey in one go, all of the investment in infrastructure and support industries, and the consequent employment, was to be lost. So it was decided that all transatlantic flights into Ireland had to land at Shannon before flying on to Dublin. This put up costs and flight times and caused national debate over the sanity of such a formality just to keep local industry happy. In 1993 a compromise was reached whereby all 747s are parked and maintained at Shannon, start their journey there and go to the United States via Dublin. Now, the only international flight which uses Shannon is the Aeroflot flight to Cuba.

Despite these difficulties Irish tourism is flourishing. In an overpopulated and polluted Europe Ireland can seem like heaven to the many Europeans that visit. Ireland still has hedgerows with wild flowers growing in them, fish in crystal clear streams, acres of unpopulated fields to put up a tent and any number of people opening new tourist developments in order to make a quick tourist dollar.

Many tourists in Ireland are backpackers who spend their summers discovering the glories of the Irish way of life.

The burgeoning industry of establishing 'interpretive centres' and 'heritage centres' around points of historic interest or natural beauty is now being viewed as a threat to the beauty of the country. Ireland is in danger of becoming a huge theme park – Hiberno-Disneyland – at the expense of its soul. It sometimes seems that every county is jumping on the bandwagon and opening farms to the public with kiddie's zoos and playgrounds and picnic sites and fields of barley planted for effect rather than the eventual product. Raths are opened up and dug out to show the public how the Celts built their homes, crumbling ploughs are polished up and stuck on display and ancient ruins deconstructed and put up again in theme parks dedicated to showing people how the Irish once lived. In one sense this is a great benefit not only to those who profit by the enterprises but to all Irish people whose old ways are fast going into decline. Without the profit motive many old mills or farms or country houses would have crumbled to nothing long ago. At the same time, however, there is a cost and something of the real attraction of Ireland is being eroded because of it.

Nevertheless Ireland attracts a fairly cultivated bunch of tourists, divided pretty evenly between the backpacking, low budget youngsters of Europe and the big spending golf and fishing tourists who stay in the big hotels and bring their hunting rifles with them. The least attractive element, and they pay for their lack of imagination by getting the worst deal, are the tour buses of many nationalities who crowd in and out of their buses. At some stage in their itinerary they don a green hat or cap, carry an imitation shillelagh that will soon break, and trundle from one heritage centre to another. Do they ever experience a good night's crack in a tiny village pub or wander along a country road taking in the colour of the mountains and the silence of high places? The hectic pace of the tourist on a two-week tour of Europe somehow just doesn't allow time to experience the unique nature of Ireland but the longer term stayers have at least this opportunity and perhaps much more in store for them.

National Industries

Like other small countries whose basic industries might never have
got off the ground if left to themselves, Ireland in its early years as an
independent state set up several state industries, not as a matter of
political belief but just out of a pragmatic need to put money where
it would do most work. Nowadays the Electricity Board, Aer Lingus,
Bus Eireann, RTE (the television and radio company), Irish Steel,
Coilte (the forestry development company), the Post Office, the
Agricultural Credit Corporation (a banking system dedicated to
financing agriculture), Bord Na Mona (the peat production company)
and the National Stud are all owned or partly owned by the state.

The state industries employ 72,000 people. They are nowadays
run by professional people for salaries rather than friends of the party
in power at the time. Ireland is closely watching Britain's efforts at
privatising its national industries with an eye to following suit. The
national airline is overpriced, electricity costs are high and the bus
service although cheap and efficient is restricted, and anyone who

sends a son or daughter to school on one of its crumbling school buses knows the condition of some of its less prestigious services. In very recent years the state run industries have encountered some serious problems in terms of the divided loyalties of some of its executives, many of whom also run related industries. Some of the scandals connected with the purchase of property and the sale of industries have become subjects for national debate.

Foreign Industry

In order to attract foreign companies to an island which sits hundreds of miles off the coast of Europe, physically isolated from its nearest western neighbour, various governments have introduced measures such as tax relief and subsidies to encourage foreign companies to settle in Ireland. The schemes were very successful and by 1991, 50% of people in manufacturing industries worked in foreign owned firms. Electrical engineering, computer hardware, and pharmaceutical firms, all businesses which need little major investment, set up in Ireland. They were attracted by the financial incentives and by the educated, literate and English speaking workforce. Although the policy has created jobs they are expensive ones in terms of lost tax on the businesses that set up. Also, firms with no connection to Ireland beyond the tax incentives tend to move out quickly as soon as profits fall, creating a highly unstable environment.

UNEMPLOYMENT

Southern Ireland currently has a population of around 3.5 million. This high a population figure was last reached around the end of the last century just before the big twentieth century emigration period began. The increase is due partly to returning emigrants, partly to labour shortages in the traditional places Irish people found work and partly due to the immigration of Europeans and other nationals. The increase in population figures puts pressure on the unemployment figures. There might be more jobs in Ireland each year but they have

Small pubs like this one abound in every village, providing a good income and employment for their owners.

to be shared between a growing number of people. Currently the unemployment rate hovers around 20% of the labour force, that is about 300,000 people. This does not include people on social employment schemes, retraining schemes or wives of unemployed men.

Many people, including the Protestant Dean of Christ Church Cathedral, believe that if Ireland's population increase matched that of its European neighbours the unemployment rate would be virtually nil. Currently the birth rate is falling steadily and when the current pre-schoolers reach the labour force, and if current employment rates stay the same, unemployment will be the lowest in Europe. Ireland has comprehensive unemployment assistance programmes on a par with other European countries. An unemployed family with two children would receive about I£120 per week, help with rent or mortgage interest repayments, free health care and various other types of assistance such as free travel to school, grants for clothing and so on. That equation often puts the unemployed into the poverty trap. It is barely enough to live on and yet the unemployed are often disinclined to seek work because they would lose at least some of their benefits.

The inner city housing estates, particularly in Dublin, show ample evidence of the poverty of some Irish families and crime rates and drug abuse are rising to match the new numbers of unemployed young people. 23% of people live at or below a level which is 50% of the average family income of Europe, while over a million Irish people live at a level below 60% of the average European income. On the whole the Irish seem to accept these fairly shocking statistics with a great deal of calm. Many women who are unemployed give much of their time to charity work or run crèches or help in schools. The men perhaps fare worse than the women since those roles are traditionally accepted as women's work. The pub, watching the racing or hurling on television and doing whatever bit of handy work on the side is available gets many unemployed men through the day.

IRISH TIME WARPS

If the Irish have taken a precise language such as English and given it a special dimension all their own then their use of time and time keeping is equally creative. In Ireland there seem to exist two different time schemes. One, which controls the arrival of buses and trains and television programmes is decidedly European. It can be positively stunning to be standing on a deserted country road having seen no traffic for an hour and convinced that the bus will never be on time only to have it roll up at the exact minute (well thereabouts anyway) that it is supposed to. Banks open and close at regular hours, libraries likewise. Offices, in the city at least, can be relied on to be open when they are supposed to.

Then there's the other kind of Irish time which is perhaps most typified by the closing hours of some rural pubs. This is the one where a friend arranges to meet you somewhere at eight o'clock and turns up two hours later with no idea that there might be anything wrong with that. You were in the pub, there was a lot of good stuff to drink and other people to talk to so why worry? Or perhaps the telephone engineer who is to arrive on Thursday morning comes the following Monday afternoon.

Everyone has anecdotes about missing, delayed or never-did-arrive deliveries, workmen or visitors. Of course this happens in other countries too but only in Ireland is it handled with good grace and a cheerful attitude. Having an apoplectic fit one day at a firm, which had yet again failed to deliver something I'd bought almost a month before, I could hear genuine surprise in the voice at the other end of the telephone line. Why, it seemed to be saying, was I so annoyed? The delivery would get made eventually – for this was the sub-text – no harm was coming to me in the meantime. I'd lived all these years without whatever it was, why worry about a few days more? And this phenomenon doesn't just work against the consumer. The same delay can often occur with bills. I have had to go into shops and ask them to send me bills that they've forgotten about.

On Time and Some Other Time

Basically Ireland seems to exist along two time-frames. In one, business carries on as it does everywhere else, efficiently and with all due respect to the local bureaucracy, necessary deadlines and need for payments. In the other time-frame the old Ireland exists, where there is all the time in the world to do things and why hurry if there's something better to be doing?

Both the Irish Electricity Board and Irish Telecom have introduced a raffle into their bill paying schemes. If bills are paid within a certain time the customer is automatically entered into a raffle and can win a car or other goodies. This isn't because people are reluctant to pay their bills but because no-one sees any hurry in doing things like that unless they see some incentive such as the chance to win a car. If you are Irish or have lived in the culture for a long time any other way of existing probably seems quite outlandish and unnecessarily fussy, but discovering this aspect of Irish life can be very frustrating for newcomers especially other western Europeans, who first of all see only the similarities with their own country and only later begin to realise that a different mind set affects people's actions in Ireland.

These two time-frames sometimes run into each other catastrophically and occasionally invade each others' private space. In most schools around the world timekeeping is a question of pupil discipline. If you are late you are in trouble. Not so in West Cork where everyone understands that the bus driver may be delivering a calf before he sets out on his bus route, or that pupils may have to bring in the cows for their father one morning, or a slight frost on the road makes it impossible for the children to get in before lunch time. If there is a big hurling match during a school day an amazing number of reasons suddenly arise as to why pupils can't make it to school that day. Again you might have waited ten minutes outside a shop for the lunch hour to end only to go on waiting longer because the shopkeeper met someone on his way back and had to stop for a chat.

For me the worst time warp of all in Ireland occurs at supermarket check-outs. They have to be the most boring places in the known universe. All over Europe time and motion experts dedicate themselves to preventing consumer fatigue by shortening check-out waiting times. In Ireland you must pray that there hasn't been a wedding or a funeral in town lately or some other thing that the check-out person and the six customers in front of you have to discuss. If you do pick a line where the check-out person knows three or four people in front of you do try to smile while you watch her hand hover in the air over the can of peas while she listens to the latest on Maura's lumbago or the pilgrimage to Knock. Since everyone else there expects a long wait and is probably striking up a conversation with the complete stranger next to them anyway, anyone who just wants to get through the check-out and get on with their lives is definitely antisocial and deserves to be held up for even longer. In fact good manners dictate that you in your turn should find something nice to talk to the check-out person about. Otherwise it would suggest that they were just a menial and you didn't care about them. In a metaphysical sense, supermarket check-outs must be the most alien thing about Ireland that I have come across. No-one in their right mind wants to spend their day queuing in a supermarket and yet all the rules of Irish good manners dictate that the whole process must be carried out with politeness and respect for the person at the counter and in Ireland that means having a good chat with them.

Business Hours

In most fast paced cities the idea of closing the shop or business for an hour and a half at the very peak time of business would seem ludicrous. When are the most people popping into shops or offices during the day? During their lunch break of course. Not so in Irish towns where for an hour or even 90 minutes every lunch time most shops and offices close. In many ways this must be one of the most civilised things about Ireland. Lunch time means just that. Everyone closes up and goes off for lunch to a pub or the park or a cafe. This is not the case in Dublin or Belfast and not generally the case in Cork, Limerick and Galway but it is a feature of life in smaller towns.

The big stores no longer close for lunch. As in most other places staff take their lunch break in shifts and no-one notices the difference. This can have an interesting effect on a small town. On a busy Fairday it will be thronged with people all bustling about with sheep and horses for sale in the town square along with stalls selling all sorts of stuff. Cars will be double parked alongside delivery vans shunting their way through streets which were never intended for this volume of traffic. Then all of a sudden the clock strikes one and everyone disappears into the nearest pub. The blinds are pulled down in the shops, the banks close their doors, the stalls shut up shop. Only the pubs and restaurants are doing any trade. At around two thirty or thereabouts things start to move again but they never really get back to the businesslike nature of the morning. It could be the hour and a half in the pub that is responsible for the new, more mellow afternoon atmosphere.

Similarly, Ireland has an ancient tradition called half day closing. On one day a week all the shops shut at one o'clock and do not open again. This is most likely because most shops in Ireland are small and employ few people and whose working hours are restricted. Whatever the reason it fits in perfectly with Ireland's very laid back attitude to business in general and daily trade in particular. Business is all right but there are so many other good things to do.

THE BLACK ECONOMY

It may sometimes seem that much of Irish daily life functions on a kind of barter system, particularly in the countryside. It would be difficult in rural areas to survive without the help of neighbours and a complex system of cooperation exists which no one calculates but which seems to work quite well. Lifts to town, help on the farm, lending farm equipment, looking after children, work in the church, a hand in the shop or behind the bar if things get difficult are all done because each person knows that they too will need the support of their neighbours sooner or later.

Unpaid or undeclared work of this nature is probably a way of life in many societies. A carpenter or handyman does work for his neighbours and knows he can call on help or the price of a pint or so when he needs it. The black economy often extends into quite illegal areas in Ireland with people supplementing their welfare payments with work or even occasionally supplementing their undeclared work with welfare payments. The welfare officers are quite aware that sometimes people are forced into these measures to stay alive and have developed certain schemes designed to help people into proper work in this way. Individuals can arrange with the welfare office to begin a business, say open a shop, while still receiving their welfare cheques. They are allowed a period of time to become solvent all the while guaranteeing that they survive at least with their welfare cheques. In this way the state is recognising that the black economy exists and tries to use it to improve people's employment chances.

BUSINESS METHODS

In recent years Ireland has been a little rattled by emerging stories of corrupt business practises but in the main Irish business methods conform more or less to the European standard. If there are differences they are probably in the lack of formality in Irish life. First name terms are the norm as is relatively casual dress in business. Women are still quite rare at the higher levels of industry and although many women have set up small businesses they are usually in traditional female areas such as childcare, catering and creative fields.

As in politics people tend to take their business to someone they have links with rather than get lots of proposals and choose the best one. When individuals seek tradesmen to do work for them it is not that unusual to arrange the work without asking for an estimate of the cost. To ask is almost insulting to the person with whom you are doing business since it suggests that they are doing the work for profit and not because they are your friend. Irish people tend to seek consensus rather than dispute something, so often negotiating a price is avoided. At a business level of course things are a little more formal than that but the feeling I think remains, that business arrangements depend a lot more on individual relations and trust than they would do in Britain or the United States.

Beyond that proviso business methods are quite in keeping with those of the rest of Europe. Irish people would not feel insulted or bribed by being taken to dinner or to the pub to discuss business although expensive gifts might become embarrassing. Time keeping for business meetings comes nearer the European norm of actually keeping meeting times fairly accurately, although no-one will feel aggrieved if there are unavoidable delays.

Chapter Nine

THE LURE OF THE LAND

WHY DO YOU WANT TO MOVE TO THE CITY?

The strands which bind us to our native land are many and various; we do not admit it to ourselves, for we see in them a sign of weakness, something almost to be ashamed of. It is only at the odd moment of departure or an unbidden flash of insight that we realise what love is. As the plane flies away from home we see in the coastline of Wicklow, the sandy beaches below, the vulnerability of earth before the mighty mass of the sea and the heartstrings are touched. Going away from it we are moved, touched.

—Tom MacDonagh, *My Green Age*

THE LAND

Few people in other parts of the world can really understand what the land has traditionally meant to the Irish. For centuries they fought one another over the land and then watched as the English forced their way into their country and gradually took it away, passing laws discriminating against the Irish and Catholics. The few occasions when Ireland united against the English imperialists it was usually over the question of land and most of this century's difficulties between Britain and Ireland have been over this issue. Ironically despite this strong feeling for the land millions of Irish people have had to turn their backs on the very thing they love the most and find a new life in other countries.

When Ireland gained its independence in 1922 most of the land was owned by absentee English landlords. After the Land War of the late nineteenth century Britain passed the Land Acts which gradually made owning Irish land less profitable to absentee landlords and allowed tenants to purchase their land. The state made provision for long term loans to tenant farmers and by 1914 most farmers were repaying the loans on the farms that they now owned themselves. After independence De Valera refused to pass on these repayments to the British and this was partly responsible for an economic war between Britain and Ireland which did terrible damage to Ireland's fledgling industries.

So the land means much more to Irish country people than a means of making a living. In times still within living memory neighbours, often closely related to one another, would fight and even go to law over tiny patches of land. The emotions that were once generated by this attachment to pieces of land can be seen in the movie *The Field,* based on a play by John B. Keane, where one man has rented a field from a neighbour and made it fertile by his efforts. When the field looks like being bought by an American he murders him.

In the heavily congested areas in the west of Ireland in the nineteenth century, land was reclaimed from the bare rock by drag-

153

ging up seaweed and sand and creating raised beds in which could be grown potatoes. A few fields created out of bare rock in this way could keep a family from starvation. By the twentieth century farmers had discovered the use of artificial fertilisers and drainage systems and previous bogland was being called into use. Literally every patch of surface land in Ireland that could be reclaimed was drawn into use. Even so, the land could not support the huge increases in population of the nineteenth and twentieth centuries and massive migrations took place away from the land, of those children not lucky enough to have any farm to take over or marry into.

This ramshackle old house might once have housed a family of fifteen, the cow kept in the end and the few small fields providing the family's potatoes and the landlord's barley.

The Move to the Cities

Not all of the migration from the rural areas of Ireland has been to other countries. The population of the cities of Ireland, especially Dublin, has grown steadily since the nineteenth century and as Ireland's tiny industries began to get underway after independence the move to the cities began in earnest. For a while the industrialisation of the country was halted by De Valera's vision of a self sufficient rural population living on tiny farms, then by the economic war with Britain and again by World War II. But the postwar economic boom found its way even to Ireland and from the 1950s those who didn't go abroad and didn't inherit the farm went to Dublin.

Dublin meant jobs and freedom from restrictions and dances and the cinema and by the 1960s there was television, cars and perhaps a husband with a good white collar job. Farming remained a low income job and gradually the feeling that the land provided the only kind of living disappeared. In rural Ireland marriage was undertaken late in life, often at age forty for the man. More girls left the countryside and gradually all of those forty year old men found that young women were less available. Bachelor farmers didn't marry, produced no heirs and rarely would a city nephew, used to city ways, be interested in taking up the long day of the farming life.

All over Ireland elderly farmers are gradually retiring and marginal land is abandoned while the better farms are bought up by neighbours or by blow-ins. The tiny village schools are growing too small to be viable and will eventually all be gone and the children bussed into the nearest town, another disincentive for people to stay in the country. Small sub-post offices are the next to go, often taking the village shop with them. Priests are even becoming too rare for each parish to have their own so in rural areas the churches are often used only once a fortnight and the people must drive to the next village for mass. The cities have hardly benefited in relation to the countryside's loss. Even cities as small as Cork now have large suburban housing estates with all the isolation and anonymity of other countries'

The morning rush hour in Dublin. During the twentieth century Ireland has undergone massive population changes resulting in a shift away from the rural areas, either overseas or to the cities.

suburbs. In Dublin unemployment is high and crime, although very low by western standards, is on the increase. Everyone now has a tale about mugging or joy-riding. The fact is that over the last forty years or so Ireland has undergone massive social change closely connected with this move from a stable rural population to a mobile city population. It has been accompanied by very altered feelings towards religion and the priesthood which for many years determined the behaviour of the whole population and now no longer does. Property and land is now an indicator of social status rather than an extension of a man's soul and is no longer worth killing for.

IRISH HOMES
City Houses

Just as it does in the rest of Europe, the house a person lives in, its location, design and decoration says much about that person's social class and aspirations. After World War II, as people's incomes and aspirations rose, the types of houses being built altered to suit the higher incomes of their buyers. Houses set away from the road, detached or semi detached with large gardens, an attached garage, central heating and above all modern design were much more in demand than the old Georgian terraces of the city centre. As a result, traditional architecture gave way to the functional, at a cost in terms of urban aesthetics.

Dublin's city centre in particular was quite beautiful with its rows of elegant four-storey terraced houses. In the property boom of the 1970s most of these were cleared away to make way for office blocks or shopping centres. They were old, admittedly, and would have needed huge investments to bring them up to modern standards but for many people they remained a symbol of the British occupation of Ireland.

Many historic buildings disappeared during the 1970s, including the house in Eccles Street where the fictional character Leopold Bloom was supposed to have lived. Many people, particularly the builders of heritage centres, have since regretted its destruction. The front door has, however, been saved and currently graces the wall of a pub in Dublin.

In London the old Georgian and Victorian houses were recognised as sound investments and their value in areas around the city centre rocketed while in Dublin similar houses were being swept away as the middle classes moved out to estates in Blackrock or Donnybrook. In the 1990s this has reversed and developers are seeing the value of old buildings. The city centres of Cork and Dublin are gradually being repopulated as old warehouses and buildings, so long abandoned, are being renovated and converted into apartments.

These well preserved Georgian terraces are some of the few that have survived the onslaught of modern city architecture.

Country Houses

In the countryside all over Ireland similar changes were taking place as the income from farming rose during the 1970s. The old farm houses were abandoned or converted for the relatives from America to live in and beside them, all over the west of Ireland particularly, sprung up bungalows. House building companies boomed and had a range of bungalow designs on offer with hard wood windows, little sitting rooms and fitted kitchens. Many of them were, and still are, grotesquely ugly compared to the farmhouses they replaced.

The older houses were built into sheltered spots among the fields with the front of the house facing south to catch the sun and the gable end windowless as it faced the south easterly winds. Small windows fitted into thick walls. They were of a simple design, one room providing the main living space and dominated by the huge hearth-place where all the heat and much of the light was produced. All of the cooking went on there in pots of water drawn from a well outside. Those that were renovated had back extensions added where bathrooms and toilets were built and a kitchen with a stove and plumbing. Windows were replaced and doors and big solid fuel cookers replaced the open fires. The wave of bungalow building finally slowed down as the cash began to get scarcer and bungalows were left unfinished or repossessed by banks. A drive around the countryside in Ireland can reveal some magnificent specimens of Irish kitsch with unsuitable hacienda style balconies and porches, odd looking arches leading nowhere and hideous red bricks brought in from goodness knows where.

A third type of building activity which is going on and threatens to be as obnoxious as the kitsch bungalow is the fake 'olde-worlde.' Killarney is an excellent example of this. Shop doorways spring olde-worlde signs, wooden doric pillars and funny little pebble glass windows. Expensive imported stone is used to recreate old cottages for tourists to take tea in. Cute rows of whitewashed cottages spring up offering self catering accommodation.

A modern bungalow. This one is quite modest in design but some are almost gothic in their decoration.

More interesting but still an oddity are the buildings designed to go back to Ireland's furthest roots. A set of buildings in Dublin known as 'the bunkers' by locals are obelisk-like concrete buildings intended to recall the dolmens, ancient burial places of the Bronze Age. A similar effort can be seen in many places around the country in churches and other public buildings. One is the public library in Bantry, County Cork which is built in the shape of a dolmen but has the characteristic 1970s concrete style about it.

One of the most active industries in Ireland is tourism and the effects of investment in tourism can be seen all over Ireland in the recreation and renovation of old buildings. Ruined beetling mills in the North are being brought back to their original condition while others become conference centres or art galleries. Ardfert Cathedral in County Kerry, destroyed during the sixteenth century is in the process of restoration, not to return it to its original use but to become an interpretive centre.

The Great Houses

As successive English monarchs parcelled up the land and handed it out to their loyal subjects, each new member of the landed gentry felt the need to build themselves a grand house to suit their station in life. Many of these houses became the object of attacks during the Black and Tan War and the following civil war. Stuck in odd places, behind high crumbling walls with the crows nesting in their roofs, they make the countryside picturesque and indicate something of the life that their owners must have once led.

Those that have survived all the troubled times are crumbling also unless their owners have found some way of making a living from their grandeur. Many are opened to the public but summer visitors are hardly enough to pay for the upkeep of some of these old houses. Others have been bought by wealthy blow-ins and are private homes.

Dunclue Castle, County Antrim. This fortified sixteenth century house was owned by a Planter family.

A large number are small and very exclusive hotels with the grounds converted into golf courses. They often have excellent salmon fishing as the men who originally built the houses would have made sure that their grounds included a good river.

One, in County Kerry, is now a youth hostel while others have turned the grounds into model farms or museums or even small businesses. Others are still somehow owned by the original family. One of these is Tullynally Castle in County Meath where the Earls of Longford still live. The castle is open to the public for a brief period each year and the perfectly preserved old kitchens, the ermine lined crowns sitting about on sideboards and the other beautiful artifacts give some indication of the luxury in which the old landed gentry once lived. In many cases some of these old houses bankrupted an entire generation of the family, such as Coole House in Northern Ireland, where it took several generations to complete the house and where some of the rooms were never furnished because of the huge expense involved.

All of these houses had great gardens designed by architects to show off the surrounding countryside to its best. Many of the keen gardeners of the time took part in the Victorian craze for exotic plants and discovered that the mild climate of Ireland provided an excellent home to many foreign plants that could not thrive in the colder climate of England. Many of these gardens still exist especially in the south west and it is possible to see huge groves of bamboo, tree ferns, exotic trees and many other plants that would more commonly be seen in tropical climates.

Gardens have always been important in Ireland whether the space available was big or small. The garden in a small holding was always the place where the family's food was grown as well as where any flowers could be cultivated. Herb gardens were kept by most families and in days now long gone flax would be grown and coloured with dyes found in the garden and grown for that purpose.

EMIGRATION

For Ireland, emigration has been a way of life for almost two hundred years. Emigration began as a response to the sudden and dramatic increase in population in Ireland which began with the peace following the Jacobite wars. The price of grain rose all over Europe and concurrent with that the potato was discovered to be a highly productive crop. Tenant farmers could raise cash with grains and feed their families on the potato. Labour to work in the grain fields became important. And so the population rose with the absence of armed men roaming the fields, improvement in the diet and the need for more labourers. In 1800 the population stood at five million. Forty years later it stood at eight million plus. There was little industry beyond farming and severe congestion on the land. The response of small numbers was to emigrate, chiefly to Britain and North America. Then in 1842 the potato crop failed, followed by another failure in 1846.

The Potato Famine

By February 1847 the workhouses and streets of the towns were full of starving and dying people. If they did not die of hunger they were taken by typhus or cholera. In those days emigrant ships only made the journey in the summer months and by summer 1846 huge numbers were making their way first to Liverpool and from there to Canada, the cheapest route to North America. By 1847 the so called coffin ships had begun departing from Cóbh in County Cork and Tralee in County Kerry. In 1847, 100,000 destitute Irish sailed for Canada from Liverpool alone. It is estimated that one fifth of them died on the journey. By 1851 about a million people had at least begun the journey to a new life in the United States.

After the Famine

In the post-Famine years Ireland once again recovered some economic stability. The great purge of people from the land meant that farms were now bigger and more economically viable. In Ulster there was an economic boom in the linen industry and the fledgling engineering and shipbuilding industries, provided employment for a new urban working class. The surplus population now regularly made its way to the new worlds. By 1870 three million Irish people lived abroad, while six million lived at home. Three fifths of the emigrants lived in the United States, one quarter in Britain and one thirteenth in each of Canada and Australia.

Half of every generation left the country, ensuring a continual decrease in population. Unlike in the Famine years, when whole families huddled in the cargo bays of ageing cattle ships, the emigrant group now consisted of those just coming into the labour market. Men and women emigrated in equal numbers in most years although often the numbers of women was higher than men. Women were preferred as cheaper sources of labour and as wives for the pioneers. The highest emigration was from the west of Ireland but all classes and religious groups felt the loss. The result was a high population of older people.

Once again family size began to increase as the money sent back to support the family from the emigrants became increasingly important. The more children who emigrated from the family the higher the chance would be of a constant source of support and funding for further emigration. By the beginning of the twentieth century about a million pounds a year found its way back to Ireland from the United States alone. The pattern emerged of one son of an average family of six children inheriting the farm while all the others left and that pattern continued well into the 1960s. So much so that by 1911 over a quarter of men over fifty had not married. Of the generation born between 1931 and 1941, 80% emigrated.

Recent Emigration Trends

During the brief economic boom of the 1960s emigration slowed down to the point where in some years there was a net immigration as emigrants returned home. During this time the United States altered its emigration laws to put a quota on the number of Irish people allowed work permits each year. At the time this was not considered a difficulty by a government convinced of a permanent economic upturn and an end to emigration. But the good years were not to last. Emigration took off again in the bad years of the 1980s and then fell again due to a lack of places to go rather than the attraction of jobs in Ireland. Emigration to the United States is now restricted to about 500 work permits a year and many illegal emigrants take up low paid, uninsured work in restaurants or building sites despite the fact that many of them are among the most well educated people in the world.

A Haemorrhage of Talent

Over the last 150 years Ireland has been saved from economic and social ruin by the willingness of her young citizens to leave the country and go abroad in search of a new life. But all things have their cost and the cost to Ireland, many people are saying, has been the loss of the talents and skills of those millions of young people.

All over the world, history and money have been created by the efforts and talents of Irish people. Some 40 million people in the United States alone claim Irish descent and not a few of those people are prominent, wealthy, influential American citizens. In an article in the *Irish American* in 1986, Denis P. Long, Irish American of the year, pointed out that 30% of the top American corporations are led by people of Irish descent. Meanwhile back at home Ireland's industrial revolution is still waiting to happen as the government gives out tax concessions to foreign firms willing to set up here. Perhaps it takes a certain type of person to have the need or courage to set out for a new land and it is those qualities that make the good entrepreneur.

Ireland itself is not without talent by any means but it is true that the talents of those who have remained in Ireland are literary or artistic talents rather than business ones. Over one or two generations that kind of drain on a nation's resources might not be noticed but what happens when all of the enterprising people leave over a period of two hundred years taking their gene pool with them?

Investing Her People

In Britain in the 1960s as most of Britain's top scientists left the country, having been offered lucrative jobs in the United States, Britain accepted it for what it was – a loss. It was called the 'brain drain.' In Ireland successive governments plan the economy with emigration in mind. When the visas for the United States and Australia recently started to become difficult to get the government opened up emigration offices in Europe hoping to attract Irish school leavers to try their hand in a new area. And so they are. In a speech during his 1963 visit President Kennedy described Irish emigration as the Irish 'investing her people' in other countries. Many people in Ireland feel that the investment has resulted in a net loss to the country.

But all this doom and gloom about the loss of the nation's young is offset by some of the happier aspects of emigration. When John F. Kennedy visited Ireland in June 1963 he came back as the descendant of Famine sufferers who fled their home in Wexford to start a new life in a new world. The town's authorities showed him a record of a distant cousin who had spent two months in jail for resisting a sheriff. His visit was an affirmation that Irish people could rise from poverty to the highest office in the world. He visited distant cousins in Wexford, told the assembled crowd in Galway that when they visited Washington to tell the guard at the White House where they were from and they'd get a special welcome. When he died six months later the whole nation mourned his passing, holding thousands of masses for the repose of his soul. A contingent of Irish army cadets were requested to attend his funeral which was watched via the Telstar satellite by thousands of people.

Irish Americans

Despite the fact that some Irish Americans are now perhaps ninth generation there are many societies in the United States dedicated to continuing Irish traditions, Irish newspapers and magazines and Irish sports organisations.

America has traditionally been a source of funds for the revolutionary groups in Ireland, Noraid being the most well known. A more legitimate group seeking aid and political pressure for a political solution in Northern Ireland has been a group made up of Tip O'Neil, the former Speaker of the House of Representatives, and Senator Edward Kennedy, as well as many other prominent politicians. Tip O'Neil was given honorary Irish citizenship in 1985 and he has accused British politicians of making a political football out of Northern Ireland and set up a trust to channel cash into employment generating projects in Ireland.

Support for the IRA and contributions towards its finances were fairly typical of a large number of Irish Americans who, safe from the violence, see simple solutions where none are possible. In recent years even the New York St. Patrick's Day parade had taken on political overtones with its organisers disaffected from the Irish embassy staff over support for the IRA. Since the upheavals of the seventies in the North there have been many initiatives offered by the United States in the form of aid for peaceful settlements, offers of direct intervention and aid packages linked to the various agreements drawn up between Britain and Ireland and the willingness of the Clinton administration to involve itself in the negotiation process has been a positive influence.

The less famous have also kept up their Irish connections. All over the west of Ireland the old family cottages have been taken over by summer visitors who barely remember their childhoods in the same

167

house. The old farm is opened up for one or two weeks a year and the returnees seek out their family and friends and spend a comfortable if probably wet vacation visiting the scenes of their childhood. Many still subsidise their elderly relatives or invest in small businesses for their relatives and many more come back to Ireland to eventually retire here.

GENEALOGY

After the American television series "Roots," looking up information about relatives became a popular activity and an industry has now developed around it in Ireland. There are businesses that will look up family records, hunt through graveyards and church birth and death registers and present the information and family crest.

Others prefer to do the work themselves. Recently some elderly neighbours of mine were able to show a young American the site of the home of his great grandfather who was once the village tailor. The elderly neighbour could remember his own grandfather wearing a suit made by the tailor. Irish people remember their genealogy as a matter of course and second or even third generation emigrants can often arrive in a country place to be told about their progenitors and even meet a few third and fourth cousins, just as President Kennedy did in the sixties.

Tracing Your Ancestors

If you are one of the many millions of people who can trace their ancestors back to Ireland there are several organisations which can help you find them. But the work of tracing relatives or ancestors must begin in your home country. Relatives must be consulted concerning your ancestors in your own country going back as far as the first emigrants. The place and date of their arrival is quite important as well as finding out what part of Ireland they came from. Dates of marriages, births and deaths are also very important as is religious denomination.

There are agencies and organisations in your home country that can help with this. For example in the United States, the Baltimore Genealogical Publishing Company has all the records of arrivals into New York from 1846 to 1851. Other places to look are army enlistment files, land grant records and the obituary sections in old newspapers. Similar possibilities exist in Australia and are perhaps even more useful since much emigration to Australia took place with state assistance and closer records have been kept.

Once all this information has been collected it should point back to the area of Ireland from which your relatives came. Irish surnames recur all over the island and knowing the name does not give any indication of where to start looking. All of the Republic's genealogical records are kept in Dublin either in the Registry of Births, Deaths and Marriages in Joyce House, Lombard Street East, Dublin 2 or in the Genealogical Office 2 Kildare Street, Dublin 2. This office provides a service giving help and advice on how to go about tracing ancestors for a fee of I£10. An appointment might be necessary, especially in the summer.

The National Library in Kildare Street, Dublin 2 has many old trade manuals and newspapers which can be searched if you know the trade of your ancestor. In all this you should bear in mind that birth records began in Ireland in 1864 for Catholics and about 1845 for Protestant marriages. There are also the National Archives in the Four Courts, Dublin 7, with material from 1922 and some from before that date. The archives would have copies of the 1901 and 1911 national census. It also has copies of Griffiths Primary Valuation of 1843–63 which lists the occupiers of land throughout Ireland. There are many other sources of information in the archives. If your ancestors came from one of the six counties then the Public Record Office of Northern Ireland, 66 Balmoral Avenue, Belfast BT9 6NY, holds registers of births, deaths and marriages, wills, tithe and land valuation records.

If you know the parish from which your ancestor came there are more detailed records of births and deaths held by each local parish

in the care of the parish priest. Church of Ireland records are at the National Archive and Presbyterian records have been collected together by the Presbyterian Historical Society Church House, Fisherwick Place, Belfast.

Gravestones are another good source of information but they were not commonly used until the middle of the eighteenth century. Collections of gravestone inscriptions have been made for counties Belfast, Down and Antrim by the Ulster Historical foundation in Belfast, Wexford, Wicklow, Sligo and Leitrim by local historical societies and Armagh, Derry Fermanagh and Tyrone by the Irish World Organisation, 26 Market Square, Dungannon, Tyrone BT70 1AB.

If all this sounds like terribly hard work you can contact one of the many agencies which will research your family history for you. Research is usually done on a county by county basis and the Genealogical Office, 2 Kildare Street, Dublin 2, can advise on the organisation most suited to an individual's needs. One island-wide organisation is the Hibernian Research Company Ltd, P O Box 3097 Dublin 6. At best what you can hope for is a seven generation account of male ancestry. Female family lines are more difficult to trace because of name changes. In addition if you hope to visit the place of origin of your family you must give whichever company you choose between one and three months to do the research before your visit. More detailed advice on how to trace your ancestors can be found in the books listed in the bibliography.

Chapter Ten

IRISH SOLUTIONS TO IRISH PROBLEMS

If I saw Mr Haughey buried at midnight at a crossroads, with a stake driven through his heart – politically speakin' – I should continue to wear a clove of garlic round my neck, just in case.

—Conor Cruise O'Brien
The Observer, October 10, 1982

SOME RECENT ISSUES

The Irish are a self doubting and self questioning race. Many people have pointed out in regard to the Irish love of language and talking that they spend so much time in examination of the issues that they never have time to actually solve any of them. This can be seen most clearly in the national institution "The Late Late Show" on television.

"The Late Late Show" and Social Change

To a complete stranger this programme might seem an anachronism, a throwback to the television of the sixties and seventies but to the Irish it is nothing less than a force for change and a sort of mirror where they can see themselves. Not every week of course. The show is on from autumn to late spring every Friday night for an hour and a half, hosted by Gay Byrne, a now elderly gent who every year fights against suggestions that he give up the seat he has held for a couple of decades.

Most weeks the show is pretty run of the mill but every now and then an issue emerges and forces its way on to the programme and the sparks fly. I have seen some great shows where fury has raged over sex education in schools or an interpretive centre in a beauty spot. In the 1960s the show was a hotbed of controversy with people travelling to the nearest television set every Friday night to watch it and listen to guests discussing things that were hardly spoken of elsewhere. A 1993 programme on the issue of abortion could have been seriously violent if not for the highly structured format imposed on it.

What the best of the shows address is this idea of the Irish solution to the Irish problem. It suggests that regardless of law or rights and wrongs Irish problems are peculiar and can best be settled in a special, oblique and not necessarily straightforward way. The following are some of the big problems that have hit Ireland in the last few years. They have to do with political chicanery, hypocrisy, nepotism and paternalism. Unlike other countries, Ireland doesn't sweep such things under the carpet but it does have a tendency to be convinced that it'll all come right on the night.

The Priesthood

For generations the priesthood in Ireland was the most highly respected group in the land. People were half afraid of their priest, would never dare address him as an individual and gave way to him on any occasion. The priest would have the daily chores done for him, would be an essential participant in any social occasion, and had their opinions obeyed in all aspects of life. Catholic priests are voluntarily celibate. In modern times they work hard in difficult and underpaid conditions, especially those in the inner cities. Many of them have to find a balance between the needs of their parishioners and a church hierarchy which is unable to keep pace with the problems of modern life. But for generations the people of Ireland accepted what their priests told them in the sincere belief that here was a hot-line to God.

Over the years many priests have found the demands of celibacy intolerable and have honourably left the priesthood, sometimes returning to their old parishes with a new wife and children, but in recent years many scandals have emerged regarding Catholic priests all over the world, including several of the Irish clergy. Perhaps that, in a way, has made them more human and understandable to the Irish people. One story, that of Bishop Eamon Casey, is not just a bit of gossip about the priesthood, it illustrates much about the nature of the new emerging Ireland and its values.

Bishop Casey was a notable and well respected figure with a long track record of working for the poor, first of all in England, where he worked tirelessly on housing projects for his mostly Irish parishioners, and then in Ireland as Bishop of Galway. He became the central figure in the charitable organisation Trocaire and was often to be seen on chat shows giving his opinions on matters, singing traditional songs and generally being one of the guys. He drove an expensive car and had been arrested for drunk driving in Britain. He was outspoken and very conservative, opposing the divorce referendum and holding up the institution of marriage as one of the central tenets of Irish life. He proudly accompanied the Pope during his visit to Ireland.

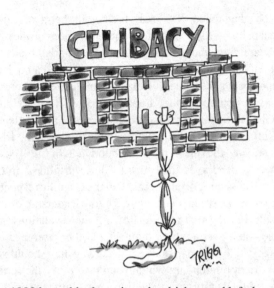

In May 1992 he suddenly resigned as bishop and left the country and the next day the *Irish Times* revealed the reason. The bishop had an illegitimate teenage son with an American woman with whom he had conducted a secret affair in 1973. For many years he had been supporting the son but refusing to recognise him and it was this refusal that made the woman and her son go public. Things got worse as the news emerged that large sums of money from the diocese funds could not be accounted for. The bishop was discovered working as a priest in a small community in South America. The funds were repaid by friends of the bishop and the bishop has since returned to Ireland for the funeral of a relative. No charges have been brought against him.

The effect of these revelations on the general public was enormous. At first the idea that he had broken his vow of celibacy, and committed adultery over a period of time, while continuing to officiate at masses, stunned many people. But this was felt to be the least of his sins. The feeling among many, revealed in a poll following the event, showed that almost 70% of Catholics thought that celibacy should be abandoned. The real feeling of betrayal came in his treatment of his own son, after his frequent sermons on the importance of good parenting, and the alleged misuse of parish funds to pay off the mother. The mother, Annie Murphy, produced a book about her affair and spent some time in Ireland publicising it where she came under severe criticism, once appearing on "The Late Late Show" where Gay Byrne made his feelings towards her very clear.

The affair has left a deep and permanent scar on the Irish people and has affected the role of the priesthood in Irish life. The long term response has been to forgive him for his worldliness in the 1970s affair but in the same poll almost 50% of the Catholic respondents said that they would have less confidence in the leadership of the church as a result. For the first time, following the revelations, the clergy remained silent over a referendum. In all other referenda the clergy had suggested to their parishioners what way they should vote. Over the Maastricht referendum which sought to ratify the further move towards political unity within the European Union the priesthood left the lay people to make up their own minds. Similarly as the law liberalising the availability of contraception passed through the Dáil in that summer the bishops remained silent, not seeking to influence public opinion on the matter.

Contraception and the Church

One of the aspects of the Catholic state in Ireland his been its adherence to the beliefs in the church regarding artificial contraception. The Criminal Law Amendment Act of 1935 proscribed the sale of all means of contraception. In 1946 the Censorship of Publications Act prohibited all literature which advocated contraception. This effectively prevented all Irish citizens, regardless of religious beliefs, from learning about or practising these methods of family planning.

Michael Solomons, a gynaecologist who has been involved in the family planning movement in Ireland for most of his working life, describes in his book, *Pro Life—The Irish Question,* the state of the thousands of women he has attended over the years, many of whom experienced multiple pregnancies, some as many as twenty. He describes the effect on women of multiple pregnancies, from high blood pressure and distension of the uterus to death caused by haemorrhaging. In 1966 the United Nations declared that "the great majority of parents desire to have the knowledge and the means to plan their families; that the opportunity to decide the number and spacing of children is a basic human right." By 1968, after another United Nations conference voted for a resolution calling knowledge and education on family planning a basic human right and of which the Holy See was a signatory, the situation slowly began to change. In Ireland many thousands of women were being prescribed the pill, ostensibly as a means of regulating their periods, another Irish solution to an Irish problem. In 1969 Ireland's first clinic for family planning was set up in Dublin to give advice to couples wanting information. It could not advertise its services or sell contraceptives but it could give them away without breaking the law. Supplies were smuggled into the country by friends of the organisation going to other countries or sent in small packets by mail order in the hope that they would not be stopped and impounded at the customs.

In 1973 a breakthrough occurred when a citizen challenged the 1935 law prohibiting the sale of contraceptives as unconstitutional and the appeal was upheld. In the same year a young senator, Mary Robinson, introduced a bill to the upper house of the Dáil in the hope of making a family planning service available to all Irish citizens. The bill was defeated but after that it was clear that changes should be made. This happened in 1980 when importation of contraceptives under licence was allowed. Condoms could be sold by chemists to married couples with a prescription. In 1985, in a celebrated court case charging a doctor with giving a patient condoms when the chemist was shut at the weekend, the presiding judge, Frank Roe said; "Anyone without condoms at the weekend will have to wait till Monday."

The laws were gradually relaxed, largely because of the threat of the spread of AIDS, until in 1993 condoms could be bought from vending machines located in suitable places. For a brief period of Irish history the law said that people could marry at sixteen but could not buy condoms until they were seventeen. The battle of the condoms is finally over in Ireland but not without much public debate and soul

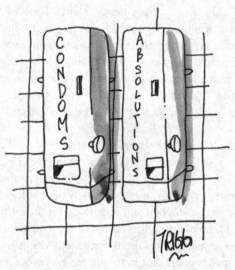

searching. Using contraceptives in order to prevent pregnancy is still a sin in the Catholic faith, although the decreasing average family size in Ireland indicates that many people are doing just that. Among the more conservative elements of society getting contraceptives is still an underhand affair, something they wouldn't like their neighbours to know about and people might go to great lengths to buy their contraceptives surreptitiously. Among young people, brought up with an awareness of the need for safe sex, the purchase and use of condoms is no longer an excuse for smutty talk or subterfuge but rather a safer way of life.

Abortion

Another thorny issue in Ireland is that of abortion. It is completely illegal in Ireland for any reason other than the threat that the mother might die if the pregnancy continue. All well and fine in a country where people genuinely believe that the foetus has a right to life from conception onwards. A situation existed, where women who could afford the journey and hospital fees simply travelled to Britain to an abortion clinic while women who had no access to information or the cost of the trip, went ahead with unwanted pregnancies. In 1983 the law regarding abortion was put into the Irish constitution by referendum. This made it possible to maintain the law while being a member of the European Union whose laws made abortion possible. But there have been some tragedies caused by this sincerely held belief and one of them hit world headlines in February 1992.

The parents of a young girl allegedly raped by a friend of her father took her to Britain for an abortion. Wishing to press charges against the alleged rapist they contacted the police and asked if foetal tissue could be used in the prosecution. The police notified the Attorney General who applied for a writ prohibiting the parents from taking the girl to an abortion clinic in Britain. They must bring her back to Ireland, foetus intact, or face prosecution. The news hit the headlines and public debate reached fever pitch. Public figures announced on television that they would go ahead with the abortion if it were their daughter and face the consequences later. The case went to the Supreme Court and again an Irish solution to an Irish problem emerged. The girl was considered by the judges to be suicidal and as such, her life was threatened and she could go ahead with the termination – but not in Ireland – she could travel to the UK for the treatment.

The judgement caused serious difficulties. If she could only travel because she was suicidal, did that mean that other women, not suicidal could not travel to the United Kingdom for an abortion as many Irish women do? If the threat of suicide meant that she was entitled to an abortion, then wasn't it possible for the abortion to take place in Ireland? And what would happen when the next girl went to her doctor and threatened suicide? Another referendum had to take place to clear up the Supreme Court decision. Public debate raged furiously while the law makers tried to find the words to enact what Irish people wanted into law – that they didn't want abortions to take place in Ireland unless the mother was going to die and that women could get abortions abroad if they wanted.

In 1993 the Irish people found themselves voting on whether Irish women had the right to travel abroad for abortions. The amendment to the constitution said that women could travel abroad and have access to information about abortion clinics in Britain. It also tried to clear up the distinction between the threat to the life and health of the mother but the wording of the amendment was so woolly that it did not solve the constitutional problem the Irish found themselves in.

In the end 38% of voters decided that women should not travel abroad for an abortion, while 40% said that women should not have access to information about abortion clinics. The proposed change to the constitution regarding the grounds for an abortion in Ireland was defeated so that the Supreme Court decision still stands. This complicated set of results means that now it is possible to supply information on abortion in Ireland and that women cannot be stopped from travelling abroad if someone suspects they intend to have an abortion. The fact that such a large number of people actually voted to stop women from travelling abroad is a telling indicator of Irish views and of the potential for division which this issue has.

Divorce

As we have already seen, the tiny number of divorces allowed in the Republic of Ireland by means of application to the Dáil were prohibited in the early years of the Republic. Divorce is not allowed in Ireland except under such complicated terms that no remarriage is allowed by either church or state. An annulment is possible which

would allow remarriage in church but would not be recognised by the state. An official state separation is recognised but remarriage under any auspices is not allowed. Irish people can seek divorce abroad but neither it nor their remarriage would be recognised by the state.

The laws regarding the ownership of property within the marriage are also rather peculiar. The wife who stays at home and does years of unpaid housework and child-rearing has no rights to the family home. Women can only claim a right to their home if they have gone out to paid work and contributed to the purchase of the house. Over 40% of Irish women work on the family farm and do more than 38 hours of farm work per week, yet if the farm belonged to the husband on marriage the wife has no rights to ownership of it. When there was a divorce referendum in 1983 many people voted against it on the grounds of the vague area of divorce settlements. If a woman were able to divorce her husband she would not necessarily have the family home as part of the settlement even if she were the custodial parent.

In 1993 an attempt was made to recognise the rights of women with regard to the family home in preparation for a second divorce referendum in 1994 but an appeal to the Supreme Court showed that the new bill was unconstitutional and it was thrown out. There are tens of thousands of people with broken marriages in the country, many having found new partners and living even more unsettled lives with no rights. 20,000 women are classified as deserted wives and are supported by the state. At this time the mood of the country favours divorce and whatever it takes to bring that about will be found somehow in the long tradition of Irish solutions to Irish problems.

A EUROPEAN IRELAND

Ireland joined the European Economic Community (EEC) as it was then called, in 1973 and the move altered Ireland's lifestyle permanently. Economically it got Ireland out from under Britain's shadow, removing the link between sterling and the punt (Irish pound) and opening up the whole of Europe as trading partners. Financially it was the goose that laid the golden egg. Part of the policy of the EEC was to bring the economic standards of all of its partner states up to the level of the wealthiest. This would create demand and stimulate trade. As one of the poorest members of the Community, Ireland stood to gain billions and it did. Between 1973 and 1991, I£14 billion flowed into Irish projects from Europe. In a country whose total annual expenditure in 1992 was only I£7.6 billion a subsidy of I£2.2 billion that same year was not to be sneezed at.

In addition there is the increase in trade that the union with Europe brings, as well as the large number of European firms that have relocated to Ireland making use of lucrative subsidies. The union has brought employment to the country, investment in roads and other infrastructure, increased Irish exports, removed the dependence on Britain and resulted in five directives altering Irish law on issues such as equal pay, access to employment, social security and labour protection. All round, Ireland's entry into the Union sounds like a wonderful success story, with Ireland now having a per capita income of 69% of the European average instead of 59% in 1973 and a trade surplus of I£500 million with Ireland's European partners.

There are drawbacks of course. One of them is that Ireland is now open to competition from her European neighbours. In agriculture for example, Irish milk farmers have been subsidised as EEC members

and protected with European cash, much of the milk making its way to the well known 'milk lakes' of Brussels. Under new legislation, however, these subsidies will go and the future for Ireland's small dairy farmers is grim. The only way to compete in an open market is to produce in bulk and that will mean the end of a way of life which has remained essentially untouched for a century or more.

On the other hand Ireland suffers from restrictions on how much it can produce in other areas. When the original entry was negotiated Irish fishing was at an all time low. Despite some of the cleanest waters in Europe and a long tradition of fishing, Ireland was given quotas for fish production which made sure that it would never be feasible to invest in the new large factory fishing ships. Consequently at seaports all over Ireland foreign fishing vessels are often tied up, selling fish to local people or even anchored offshore buying up fish from local small fishermen to take away to sell at a profit.

The Maastricht Treaty

The Irish solution scenario entered the European Union question over the Maastricht Treaty. The treaty has caused controversy all over Europe with Denmark initially voting against it in a national referendum, much to everyone's embarrassment. No-one is really too sure what the implications for the member countries are in terms of any conflict between their own laws and those of the European Union, as it is now to be called. Ireland for one would be in an unusual position concerning its policy of neutrality because its participation in the European Union now calls on it to come to the European Union's defence should the necessity arise. But the benefits to be gained in terms of the billions of pounds on offer outweighed even the issue of neutrality and Irish people voted with their wallets on the issue.

At another level it might be interesting to ask where all those billions went if a very under-populated country still has an unemployment rate of 20% and encourages its brightest and best to emigrate year after year. Much money has gone on badly needed (and in some cases not so badly needed) infrastructure. Ireland's roads are cute but painful to drive on and many improvements have been made in recent years. But another deeply felt worry in Ireland concerns the use of European money to build a tourist infrastructure. Tourism is a major growth area in Ireland and thousands of new jobs can be created in the industry but there are downsides to the Irish tourism boom.

Nouveau Tourism

A sad side effect of such a concentration on tourism is the growth of 'interpretive centres' that are springing up all over Ireland. An interpretative centre is more than just a modern expression for a museum. They break up Irish life and history into neatly packaged, user friendly and above all simplified units. Recently when such a centre was planned for one of Ireland's areas of outstanding beauty, the Burren in County Clare, outraged locals went to Brussels and demanded that the cash be withdrawn. Their argument was that the

Giant's Causeway. Behind it is a large interpretive centre – some people just visit the centre and never make the journey to the rocks.

centre would bring little or no long term work to the area but would do major ecological damage. That project was eventually stopped because of the public outcry.

Another similar project exists in County Kerry where an inaccessible offshore island, Skellig Michael, has been a site of pilgrimage and a brilliant day out for tourists for many years. Recently an interpretive centre was set up close by on the mainland and tour buses stop regularly for tourists to go into the centre, read the excellent information about the island and take a trip out to see it. But the official boats do not land on the island and many of the small boat owners who once made a living from taking tourists out to the island where they could walk about and experience the archaeological remains at first hand are losing business. So, has the centre helped the site by explaining it and keeping tourists away from the actual ruins or has it prevented visitors from going there and robbed the local people of work?

In the long term Ireland surely has to learn to do without European Union cash. Interpretive centres and roads provide short term work but what is really needed are long term growth industries, not dependent on European Union subsidies to keep them in Ireland, which will provide employment for the thousands of bright, well educated youngsters who leave every year in search of their futures.

The Beef Tribunal

For about a year or so in Ireland, every evening I would turn on the television news to hear about the former Yugoslavia or the Middle East or earthquakes and would instead hear about the Beef Tribunal. This blessed enquiry sat for over 200 days at a total cost of I£20 million, called 600 witnesses and solved very few problems.

The tribunal was brought about after a British television documentary alleged that Irish beef exporters were using fraud to obtain European Union subsidies, mishandling the beef they exported, falsifying records, paying wages secretly to avoid taxation, buying beef from non-Irish sources and using intervention beef that had already been processed and changing the markings on the beef in order to bring it up to the necessary standards. Particular companies were accused of getting political favouritism in contracts from the Irish government. Many of the sales were to Iraq which eventually refused to pay for all the exported beef and the main exporter went into debt. A lot of leading politicians called each other names. Witnesses refused to name their sources, the government of the day fell from power to be re-elected in a coalition with those who had refused to have anything to do with such a dishonest party. No definite conclusions were drawn or recommendations were made regarding business practises. The whole affair cost the country a lot of money, bored everyone silly and confirmed everyone's belief that the country was being run on an 'Irish solutions' basis.

Chapter Eleven

A BIT OF CRACK

If I make a good movie they say I'm a British director and
if I make what they think is bad one, they say I'm Irish.
—Neil Jordan
The Independent, February 3, 1993

What most of the world knows as a dangerous narcotic is in Ireland one of the best and funniest aspects of Irish life. Crack in Ireland means good fun, a laugh. People talk about doing things for 'the crack of it.' Crack can be applied to anything from teasing a friend about their new suit to something as big as the Cork Jazz Festival. Despite the advent of television the Irish still revere making their own entertainment and with an enormous amount of talent in the country this can be experienced in most places at most times of the year, if you know where to find it, from rebel songs in the local pub to village festivals and all the events of several bustling cities.

MUSIC

Ireland has a long history of music making which owes very little to other western traditions. In the old days of rural Ireland each village had its accordion player, tin whistle players and folk singers who often invented their own local songs about the people of the neighbourhood. Old people can still sing some of the songs their fathers made up about a neighbour's drinking habits or how their house was built. Topics covered included anything and everything of local interest.

There are several instruments of Irish origin which feature largely in Irish traditional music. The *uillean pipes* are a kind of bagpipe played by inflating air through a bellows and sound rather like the Scottish bagpipes but with a greater range. The Irish harp is a little less in evidence nowadays but has stood as a symbol of Irish culture for many years. The *bhrodran* is a drum made from goatskin drawn over a wooden rim and played with a double ended baton, creating a very distinctive sound. In the old days the chief means of entertainment for the young would have been a spontaneous dance called in the biggest open space, often at the crossroads of a village, where all the young people would meet, musicians would arrive and a dance would take place. Marriages would often be made at such an event. Dancing consisted of Irish set dancing, a highly organised kind of square dance without the caller. Pairs of dancers would dance in formation, changing partners and taking turns to perform highly stylised sets. This can still be seen around Ireland, is often taught at evening classes and usually crops up on television, especially in programmes like "The Late Late Show" on the nights when Irishness is being celebrated. The tourist market is filled with professionals performing these dances at banquets in old houses where traditional music can also be heard. These tend towards the "Danny Boy" sentimental area of song and, unless you particularly like them, are best avoided.

Better still are the thousands of young players to be seen nightly in any one of a thousand pubs all over the country especially at local festivals. Look out for small, badly written posters in pub windows or

Music springs up everywhere in Ireland. Busking is a popular way of making some extra money, particularly on the city streets.

ask around. Good music crops up in the least likely places. In the 1950s and sixties Ireland had its own kind of sentimental country music, big dance bands toured the country with singers who became well known nationally if not internationally. From this huge interest in dancing and music emerged bands such as The Chieftains, who play traditional music with a special touch of their own making. The Chieftains are still very much in evidence in Ireland and have made albums in China and with other big names such as Van Morrison. The Dubliners are another traditional band whose songs are a little more in the Dublin tradition and have received the peculiarly Irish honour of having had some of their verses banned.

More in line with western music are other well known Irish rock bands such as U2. Sinead O'Connor also grew to international fame, partly through her singing and partly through her ability to say outrageous things. Ireland has a long country music tradition, the kind sung by Dolly Parton or John Denver, and has its own well known singers of this style such as Daniel O'Donnel and Maura O'Connell.

DANCING

If there is one thing about Irish music and dance that is peculiarly Irish it is Irish dancing. It would be nearly impossible to spend much time in Ireland without coming across this phenomenon. It is performed chiefly by women wearing quite strictly defined costumes of a green dress covered with complex embroidery, dancing pumps and white socks and a little cloak strapped to the shoulders. The dancers dance on the spot, the chief complexity of the dance being in the footwork of the dancer. The hands are kept rigidly by the side unless needed to form an arch with another dancer and the face is quite expressionless. All over Ireland and Britain young Irish girls compete at *ardh feis* – dancing competitions where they are judged on the complexity of their footwork. The dance is quite rigid both in its style and variations, the excellence of the dance not being its originality or innovation but its adherence to given patterns.

FESTIVALS

Festivals are essentially a part of the cultural tradition of making your own entertainment. In the eighteenth and nineteenth centuries and even before that, travelling dancing masters and musicians would move from village to village giving lessons and performances, often competing with one another for the right to stay in an area and be its master. These competitions between the masters would often turn into festivals where everyone in the village with a little talent would demonstrate their ability to sing, recite poetry, dance the traditional Irish dances or play their instrument..

The Traditional

One famous harpist was Turlough Carolan who travelled around the country in the eighteenth century playing for anyone who would pay him and listen. In those days Gaelic was not seen as a symbol of republicanism and many Planters appreciated the Gaelic songs of men such as Carolan. The festival or *feis* would include singing, dancing storytelling and poetry recital competitions. James Joyce was once beaten in the singing competition in Dublin by the famous Irish tenor Count John McCormack. In modern times feis are every bit as important as they once were, although tourism is probably more likely to be keeping the tradition going than local interest in preserving the old ways.

Irish dancing, as we have seen, is enormously popular although perhaps more with the mothers, who take their daughters from one feis to another, than with the girls themselves, who quickly seem to give it up only to put their own daughters through it in the next generation. Belfast, Dublin and Cork have a feis every year and each year there is a national feis held usually somewhere in the west of Ireland which can attract 100,000 or more people. There are also festivals given over to particular aspects of Irish culture such as the Clare Festival, devoted to the uillean pipes.

The Modern

In addition, there are more modern festivals such as the enormously successful Cork Jazz Festival, which owes nothing to traditional Irish music, but is itself in keeping with the Irish ability to make a celebration out of anything. The festival lasts for about a week in October and for that time every hotel, guest-house and hostel for miles around is full with visiting musicians from all over the world and with jazz enthusiasts. Music rings out from every concert hall, meeting room, pub, and street corner and tickets for some of the more well known performers change hands at inflated prices on the street. During the tourist season every town of any size has a week of festival when a fair will visit the town, some big names in local music will be engaged and street performers of every kind can be seen. Much of this is organised to attract tourists but it does not detract from the experience of a good, well organised festival.

LITERATURE AND THE PERFORMING ARTS
The Theatre

At the turn of the century in Ireland along with the Gaelic Revival movement came a group of powerful playwrights whose plays became so controversial that on some occasions director and actors had to be smuggled out of the theatre to avoid the angry mobs outside. The Gaelic Revival brought about the establishment of the Abbey Theatre in Dublin where in 1907 John Millington Synge's play *The Playboy of the Western World* caused a riot. Nationalists objected to the hero of the play who had murdered his father. Twenty years later more riots broke out over the showing of *The Plough and the Stars* by Sean O'Casey. This time nationalists objected to the flag being carried into a public house during the course of the play and others objected to the portrayal of a prostitute on stage. From that point on a whole string of world famous playwrights emerged from Irish society, most of them preferring to live their lives outside of Ireland. They include George Bernard Shaw, Oscar Wilde, Samuel Becket and in more modern times Brian Friel, a writer from the North.

The theatre as a cultural phenomenon is alive and well in Ireland. A city as small as Cork is able to offer plays on most nights of the week even in winter and many travelling theatre groups find their way to the smaller towns. Most small towns and even villages have their local amateur theatre group who, if they don't produce the most avant-garde productions, keep alive the old plays of John B. Keane and other Irish playwrights. John B. Keane's plays are concerned with the lives of rural Irish people and in them much that is almost lost to the young generation can still be found. Going to see a play by Keane is a wonderful introduction to Irish rural life and Irish humour.

Irish Literature and Censorship

If Irish businessmen have mostly achieved greatness in the New World or in Britain, then Irish writers have for the most part followed suit. It is a great irony that if you took all the Irish writers out of the English literature courses taught in British universities there would be a significant void. Irish writers have written in English for well over a century and many have made a better job of it than their English peers. Maria Edgeworth, Kate O'Brian, Oscar Wilde, George Bernard Shaw, Brendan Behan, Samuel Becket, Seamus Heaney, Brian Friel, Jennifer Johnston, Edna O'Brien, Patrick Kavanagh and W. B. Yeats are most notable but the most famous of all Irish writers is of course James Joyce. He left Ireland partly out of a sense of being stifled and partly out of a lack of job prospects in Dublin. It is his writing rather than that of Yeats, the leading member of the Gaelic Revival and Irish senator, that has influenced later Irish writers.

Joyce was never officially banned in Ireland although it would have been impossible to buy any of his novels from reputable booksellers, who imposed their own rules about what was decent to sell in Ireland. At one stage the Censor Board, established in 1929, was banning three books a day and the list of banned material read like a reading list for any university English literature course. The censorship laws are still in existence but most of the big names are off the banned lists which concentrate nowadays on pornography or licentious material. But if the Censor Board has let up on some of the nation's most talented, there are still people who wish to control what the Irish read. In 1990 John McGahern's second novel *Amongst Women* was short-listed for the Booker Prize and received the Irish Guinness Peat Aviation Prize. He was then sacked from his Catholic school teaching post.

Roddy Doyle is one of Ireland's most famous modern writers. He wrote the book on which the successful movie *The Commitments* was based and has written several more novels since, the last of which, *Paddy Clarke Ha Ha Ha,* received the much coveted Booker Prize in 1994. It is interesting though that Roddy Doyle could not find a publisher in Ireland and was forced to publish *The Commitments* privately before having it taken up by an English publisher.

Another very Irish oversight when it comes to Irish talent was in the recent *Field Day Anthology of Irish Writing*. The Field Day Group are a group of modern Irish writers based in the North and founded by Brian Friel. They undertook to produce an anthology of the best of Irish writing which duly appeared in 1991 in three volumes. What none of the editors of the edition noticed until it was too late was that they had left out most of the major women Irish writers. The editorial board was all male and one assumes were unable to see any value in anything women had written in Ireland. A muted outcry followed the publication and a fourth volume is in preparation which will consist of all those women that somehow got left out. Many women writers have pointed out though that this in itself is perhaps even more insulting, an example of positive discrimination.

Despite this, Irish publishing is in good health with Irish people spending on average I£23 per head, per annum on books and 41% of all books sold in Ireland being published there.

The Film Industry

Perhaps because of the enormous number of Irish people living in the United States, the American film industry has on many memorable occasions reflected the American view of Irish life. This tends to be rather over sentimental with a preponderance of little people and wily locals wheedling pints out of the innocent visitor. When movies are made on location in Ireland the memory of it among local people remains long after the sets have disintegrated. In County Kerry the site where the movie *Ryan's Daughter* was filmed is now part of a tour of the area where visitors are shown the place where the village was created and the place where Robert Mitchum almost drowned. In Cong in County Mayo a small industry has evolved around the remains of the film set and locations for the 1951 movie *The Quiet Man*, filmed by John Ford and starring John Wayne and Maureen O'Hara. Less memorable both artistically and as far as the local population was concerned, was the recent movie *Far and Away* which was partly filmed in Ireland, some of Dublin's backstreets forming the location for the scenes set in nineteenth century Boston.

Ireland has, in the nineties, been the subject of a whole stream of Irish movies, made by American movie companies, following in the wake of successful films such as *The Commitments*. Other successful movies such as *The Crying Game* and *My left Foot* have also put Irish directors and actors in a position to get funding from abroad.

Ireland had its own fledgling film industry set up in the late 1950s at Ardmore, County Wicklow but apart from some minor successes it failed to flourish and state funding was removed in 1987. With the success of people such as Neil Jordan, who made several memorable films in the 1980s and won an Oscar for his screenplay of *The Crying Game,* another attempt is underway to get a film industry going. It is based in County Galway and has many talented Irish people on its board of directors.

The cinema as a form of entertainment had a shaky start in Ireland, meeting the opposition of conservative elements in Irish society, who saw it as a threat to Irish values and a film censorship act was passed in the 1920s. By the 1930s there were regular cinemas in Dublin and makeshift ones in village halls all over the country. The American movies may well have been a crucial factor in the large scale emigration that characterised the thirties and forties in Ireland. For the first time young women had a glimpse of another world and what was possible in it. By the fifties small cinemas were springing up in the smallest of places and the big movies of the time did the rounds, suitably censored of course. As the sixties progressed and television began to dominate cultural life many of the small flea pit cinemas closed and are now wholesale furniture warehouses or supermarkets but in some small towns they still flourish, showing films once or twice a week and looking more like launderettes from the outside than cinemas. In Dublin, Cork and Galway the cinema flourishes with the big old picture houses converted into small screen units. Censorship is still annoyingly present, although it was liberalised in 1964.

Wayne's World, a most innocuous film, was listed as an over 18 movie. Despite this, children watch all the violence they can handle in the security of their own homes as it is beamed in on satellite or British television, or played on their video machine.

THE IRISH MEDIA
Television

Perhaps the greatest destroyer of crack all over the world has been television. Like the cinema and much of Irish literature it too was opposed as being liable to bring about social change of an unwelcome nature. British television had been received in some parts of Ireland as early as the late 1950s but televisions were very rare indeed. In 1961 a national television station was set up. By 1967 about 80% of urban households owned a set while about 25% of rural houses owned one. 20 years later the figures had risen to 92% in Dublin and 54% in rural Connacht.

There are now two channels with very little difference between them that I can see and the promise of an Irish language channel to come. At the moment there are some Irish language programmes on both of the other channels but the language is predominantly English – American English that is. Whoever decides the programming tends to go for safe middle of the road family comedy, nonviolent films and well tried English documentaries and police thrillers. There are also some home grown soaps which fail to thrill me but are very popular. One is set in a suburb of Dublin and involves controversial topics. There are also lots of very successful television shows which are either related to the Lotto or are chat shows hosted by well known hosts such as Gay Byrne, Pat Kenny and Bibi Baskin. Both channels are commercial with English adverts dubbed with Irish accents as well as some home made local advertising.

Radio Telefeis Eirann (RTE) has come under much criticism in recent years over its broadcasting monopoly and its funding. Both channels are commercial, gaining enormous revenues from advertis-

ing but also benefit from the revenue from licence fees. Its justification of its two sources of income are that it has very high overheads, having to fund all Irish language programmes and run two orchestras. In addition it can hardly be said to be in a monopoly situation since it can only claim 36% of viewers at peak times, the others being tuned in to British television or satellite.

Radio

Radio has existed for longer than television and first broadcast from Dublin in 1926 and from Cork in 1927. After 1933 most of the country was able to tune in to the national channel. By the 1940s the radio station had its own orchestra. Programming tended to be highbrow with plays, classical and traditional music and lots of religious broadcasts. Politics rarely encroached.

In 1960 the organisation was restructured to introduce television and make it more independent of government views. Radio Telefeis Eirann was given the right to collect licence fees from viewers and listeners and to advertise. In 1972 a Gaeltacht radio station was established. By the 1980s there were thousands of small local pirate radio stations all over Ireland which were taking the more staid Radio 1 and 2FM's listeners away. In 1988 they were effectively forced to become legal by the introduction of licences for independent broadcasters and local radio now has a marginally larger audience than the two public radio stations. Radio 1 is the current affairs chat show type station with an older audience. Radio 2FM has a younger audience and more pop music.

Several big names in Ireland have daily radio shows which are extremely popular and which cover many current issues on a phone-in basis. The most popular show and one to listen to for an ear into the pulse of the nation is the "Gay Byrne Show" daily from 9.15 to 11 am. His show covers controversial issues such as homosexuality, divorce and unemployment. A particularly important radio broadcast by Gay Byrne on his morning show followed the death of a young girl in a Marian grotto in County Kerry in 1985. She died giving birth to an illegitimate child. He was besieged by letters from women who had experienced the then still stigmatised illegitimate birth. The letters were read out during the programme and had a seminal effect on public opinion. Both stations have a Dublin bias but there are now local RTE stations which have a daily airing on national radio.

Newspapers

If British newspapers are politically oriented, in Ireland their orientation for a long time had more to do with religion than politics. There is, as far as I can see, no difference between the two major political parties in Ireland except what side they fought on in the Civil War. Religion is the real dividing line on both sides of the border.

The *Irish Times* was traditionally the Protestant newspaper, although it has long been nonaligned over religious matters. Mary Robinson's first political campaign was as a sixth-former trying to get this newspaper allowed into her school library for the students to read. It is also politically nonaligned supporting neither of the two major parties. It is the most serious of the daily newspapers and contains more foreign news than the others. The *Irish Independent* is the biggest daily seller, is more politically partisan but is definitely a Catholic newspaper. It has a Sunday version, The *Sunday World*, now called the *Independent on Sunday*, which is a mild version of the British *News of the World*, full of gossip and news of the stars.

Less commonly read nowadays but once very influential is the *Irish Press* which supports Fianna Fail. It was founded by the De Valera family and Eamon De Valera, the architect of the constitution, was for a time its managing director. The publishing group produces three papers – a daily newspaper, a Sunday paper and an evening paper. The daily paper changed to a tabloid format in 1992 but this failed to prevent its plummeting sales. At about the same time the board of directors were fiercely fighting for control of the newspaper group and the matter was eventually settled by the High Court. Also available in the Republic are most of the British newspapers many of them producing a cleaned up Irish version with more Irish news and fewer exposed breasts.

Many Irish newspapers adopt a superior moral tone over the British gutter press's scandal mongering but had pretty much of a field day over a recent disclosure of a Teach Dáil being questioned by police in a known gay prostitute area of Phoenix Park in Dublin. Since 100,000 British newspapers are bought every day in Ireland compared to 350,000 Irish papers, there is a considerable Irish market for a good bit of British smut, if one estimates that each paper is read by at least two people. There are also four evening newspapers, while the *Cork Examiner* is widely read in the rural southwest of the country.

In Northern Ireland the British papers are available as well as two sectarian newspapers, the *Unionist Newsletter* and the *Republican Irish News*. There is also the newspaper of Sinn Féin and the IRA, *An Poblacht*. There are any number of regional newspapers from the *Clare Champion* to the *Kerryman* or the *Munster Express*, all of which hold considerable sway over their local Teach Dáil. Weekly or monthly papers include the *Irish Farmer's Journal* which is a very influential publication and *Hot Press,* almost as influential among its readers, the young city dwellers. *Hot Press* is music oriented but often carries articles on current issues of concern to young people. The biggest selling magazine in Ireland is the *RTE Guide*.

Reporting on Paramilitaries

Until the Major-Reynolds summit and the production of the Downing Street Document in December 1993 there was in Ireland, as in Britain, a ban on showing or reporting the words of leaders of Northern paramilitary leaders.

The ban came into being in 1971 and was redefined in 1976. It came under severe criticism from the press. The problem with the ban centres on Sinn Féin which is a legitimate political party on both sides of the border, with Teach Dáils in the Dáil and for a time representatives at Westminster. It meant that the local representative of some areas of the south could not appear on television to discuss any issue at all, be it housing, the Beef Tribunal or whatever. Also, despite the fact that they put up many candidates for election, they could not be given air time for party political broadcasts as the other parties were. To complicate the issue Sinn Féin was not banned from broadcasting in Northern Ireland where all the trouble was centred. The point at issue was the effect of silencing people like Gerry Adams. If he could never be heard in the Republic he could never be asked to justify the behaviour of the IRA. It gave Sinn Féin leaders a kind of glamour to be banned. The ban ended in 1994 after the Downing Street Declaration and its removal has really had very little impact on Irish society.

Censorship vs Crack

There definitely seems to be a split personality about the Irish. On the one hand we have the very powerful conservative elements in society which kept the swinging sixties at bay, censored much of what people in other countries saw on their screens and even allowed the local priest to control what went on at Saturday night dances. On the other there is the lively, rebellious, heavy drinking, musically talented, outgoing part of the Irish that loves anything for a laugh and especially the pleasures of the flesh. Perhaps there is even a third part of this Irishness which almost cynically exploits the other two, putting on the crack for eight weeks of the tourist season in the summer and paying lip service to conservatism in their weekly attendance at church.

Chapter Twelve

RACE, CREED OR COLOUR

Other people have a nationality. The Irish and the Jews have
a psychosis.

—Brendan Behan, *Richard's Cork Leg*

IRELAND'S ETHNIC MIX

Ireland is remarkably racially homogenous. It has been a colonised country rather than an imperial one and the policy of the imperialist power was to introduce only one group of immigrant settlers which was also racially homogenous, albeit religiously divided from its indigenous population. Unlike the situation in many other parts of the world, there has been little scope for immigration from poorer countries or any connection between Ireland and other countries to encourage large movements of people into the country.

There are small ethnic groups which can be distinguished in Ireland although they tend to remain inconspicuous minorities. It could be said that on account of this Ireland is remarkably free of racial unrest and racial prejudice. There is, unfortunately, enough sectarian unrest on the island to make up for the absence of the kind of racial conflict that erupts in some of Ireland's neighbouring countries. And paradoxically, because Ireland has remained a fairly cohesive and undivided nation – genetically speaking – there is the potential for suspicion of racial or ethnic differences. A black person appearing in rural Ireland could get stared at openly simply because not many black people are seen outside of the cities.

Immigration

Immigration is restricted in Ireland. European Union citizens may come and go and work as they please but other nationals may enter only on a tourist visa or they must apply for a resident's permit and a work permit. Work permits are very restricted and an employer must prove that there is no Irish or European Union citizen capable of doing the job before a permit will be allowed. Anyone who has lived in Ireland legally for five years may apply for citizenship. There are also complicated rules regarding the citizenship of parents or even grand-parents that allow people to apply for citizenship.

There are thought to be about 5,000 illegal immigrants in Ireland, mostly from countries in Asia, chiefly Hong Kong. Many of them arrive on a visitor's permit and stay with relatives, working illegally in restaurants or the family business. They can claim no employment assistance, risk deportation if they visit a doctor and are liable to exploitation from their employers. There is no way at present that illegal immigrants can get immunity even if they have married and have Irish children. About 1,500 foreign work permits are issued each year mostly to people from Pakistan and India. There are no figures for the numbers of European Union citizens living in Ireland but it is high, especially in the west of Ireland where many small businesses are French, Swiss or German owned, as their owners take up European Union subsidies for settling in Ireland. Most work permits are granted to doctors and nurses who spend short periods in Ireland doing an internship. Anyone who can establish their credit to the tune of I£150,000 can settle in Ireland and start up a business.

Travellers

The position of Travellers in Ireland is a difficult one and raises many issues, not the least of which is the Irish claim to ethnic and racial tolerance. Travellers make up about 0.5% of the total population of the island, about 22,000 people; they are a tiny minority but a very visible one. Their origins are unknown. It is very unlikely that they have any ethnic connection with the Romany Gypsies of Europe or America although their lifestyle was very similar in times past. They are Catholic and ethnically indistinguishable from their settled neighbours. Within a generation of a Traveller family taking settled accommodation they are no different in any way from other Irish people. It is possible that they are the descendants of the dispossessed peasants of the eighteenth century or later, or that they descend from one of the Celtic travelling clans – the Bards perhaps.

As late as the 1960s they travelled around the country in hand painted, horse drawn wooden caravans. These can still be seen around the country but are more likely to contain tourists on holiday than travelling people. Modern Travellers live in site caravans that have to be towed from one site to another by lorry. They are often attractively decorated but with chrome nowadays and often with satellite aerials on the roof. At one time each Traveller clan had their own county and rarely moved out of it. The Carty's were Clare Travellers, the Wards from Galway and the Maughans from Mayo.

Nowadays most Travellers are more settled, living on illegal fixed sites as long as they can before being evicted or living in established sites with a degree more comfort but much local opposition. In the past their dress was distinctive with the women wearing bright plaid shawls rather than the black ones that older settled women wore. Modern Travellers dress in a similar way to regular country people. They had a secret language or argot called Shelta which used English, Irish and some made up words.

They were traditionally tinsmiths and mended pots, sharpened knives and bought and sold things. This aspect of their lifestyle remains and modern Travellers often have a collection of elderly and

Have satelite dish – will travel. This caravan is home to a Traveller family and boasts many modern conveniences, including international television reception.

207

antique bits and pieces set out at the roadside that they have bought from houses that they visit around the country. Horse trading was a natural part of their livelihood since they used horses to draw their caravans and this too is still a part of some Travellers' interests and occupations.

Mending pots has been replaced by scrap dealing and this brings us to one of the areas where Travellers and their settled neighbours clash. Dealing in scrap metal often leads to large amounts of junk lying around the site of any Traveller settlement. It is an eyesore and tends to reduce the value of houses in the locality. Consequently most people tend to put up a great deal of resistance when local councils decide to build proper sites for Travellers. Besides the junk, many people consider Travellers to be criminal in intent, unruly in their behaviour, drunk for much of the time and dirty. Poorer Travellers are called lazy and are accused of scrounging off the state while the richer ones are suspected of making their money through crime, despite the many government inquiries into the lifestyle and criminal participation of the Traveller population which show this is not true.

All over Ireland huge rocks can be seen on the wider grass verges to prevent caravans stopping, and signs prohibiting caravans are not aimed at tourists in their campers but at Travellers. Sites with washing facilities are due to be built but often when a site is designated local people campaign against it. In Belfast one such site which cost £20,000 to build was destroyed by local residents. Another cause for complaint about the Travellers is the number of children who beg on the streets of major cities.

Conditions for Travellers can be very harsh because few sites, even those designated by local councils, have facilities like water, sewerage systems or rubbish collection. Travellers have large families and their children suffer academically from their constant movement, and are constantly at risk from traffic. Their life expectancy is lower than the average for Ireland. Males can expect to live about ten years less than their settled peers while for women the figure is twelve years less. The infant mortality rate is eighteen deaths per thousand as opposed to the national average of seven per thousand. Only about 1,200 families still travel about, the rest being either settled in houses or on fixed sites.

There are of course two sides to every argument and it is important not to be taken in by the romantic notion of the 'nomadic gypsy.' Travellers' sites are a mess, they do create an eyesore and a health hazard in towns desperate to attract tourists. In my local area a Traveller family has settled on a site that the local council wanted to build into a children's playground so all work has stopped while negotiations take place. When the Travellers went to the local community centre for help in writing to the council putting their case for a Travellers site there instead, the people working there who helped them were criticised by their neighbours for giving the help.

Legislation is currently under way which will recognise Travellers as a distinct nomadic ethnic group and guarantee their right to travel but it is more in the area of social acceptance than legislation that the changes need to be made. The problem will not go away with the legislation. The work that helped shape the Travellers' lifestyle has basically gone with the invention of plastic and the new prosperity that allows people to throw away broken saucepans and buy new ones. Where the Travellers settle in houses their neighbours, even ex-Travellers, don't accept them easily. It is the classic situation of everyone wanting something to be done about it but not near them.

Ireland's Jews

Judaism has a long history in Ireland. The *Annals of Innisfallen,* an ancient Gaelic poem about the political events of the time and written in 1077, records the visit of five Jews to the High King of Ireland at Limerick. Major migrations of Jews into Ireland followed the expulsion of all Jews from Spain and Portugal in 1492. They mainly settled in communities around the south coast of the island. The earliest sign of a sizeable settled community in Ireland is in the Jewish cemetery which was established in Cork City in the early 1700s. A Dublin community was established in the 1660s with a prayer room and a cemetery so numbers must have been substantial. More communities are recorded in the town records of Derry, Lurgan, Limerick and Waterford. A Belfast community was in existence in 1864 and the foundation stone of its synagogue was laid in 1871. In the Napoleonic wars of the early 1900s more Jews, this time from France, arrived in Ireland but the biggest wave of immigration occurred between 1880 and 1910 following the pogroms in Lithuania and Russia.

For a time in the late nineteenth and early twentieth centuries Dublin, Belfast and Cork had large thriving Jewish communities. Cork has an entire area where only Jewish people lived called Jewstown. The streets would have held kosher shops, ritual bath houses and synagogues. Many non-Jewish people in the cities can remember with affection buying bagels or other Jewish delicacies from the local stores. Numbers of Jews in Ireland have declined since then through emigration and assimilation into mainstream religions and the Jewish population figure now stands at about 2,000, mainly in Dublin, Cork and Belfast.

The Jews have not had an easy time of it even in tolerant Ireland. In Limerick in particular they met a great deal of prejudice with priests preaching from the pulpit to their parishioners not to frequent Jewish shops or use Jewish workmen. The Jewish cemetery there was allowed to fall into ruin as the Jewish community left for other areas but it has recently been restored.

Ireland's Jews live an inconspicuous life in small communities where family life revolves around the synagogue. Jewish children mostly attend Catholic schools although there is a school for Jewish children of all ages in Dublin where the emphasis is on religious study. Jews are not an evangelistic group and do not try to make converts to their religion and the emphasis has been mostly in the other direction. Many young Jewish people find husbands and wives from the general community where Catholics are expected to insist on the children of a mixed marriage becoming Catholic. Their dress, on religious occasions at least, distinguishes them from their Catholic neighbours and some children report a very mild form of abuse aimed at them but Catholic-Jewish relations remain good.

In Ireland Jewish people are not a race of immigrants living a separate existence in a foreign country. They are Irish first and Jewish second. They support the Irish football team, learn Irish at school, play Gaelic football and do all the things that other Irish people do.

Considering their small numbers in the country the Jewish community takes an active part in Irish public life. The Lord Mayor of Belfast in 1899, Daniel Joseph Jaffe, was Jewish and the Lord Mayor of Cork in the 1970s, Alderman Gerald Goldberg, was also Jewish. In recent years three Teach Dáils were Jewish; Ben Briscoe of Fianna Fail, Alan Shatter of Fine Gael and Mervyn Taylor of Labour. The most famous Irish Jew of all must be the fictional one – Leopold Bloom – the protagonist of James Joyce's novel *Ulysses*. Joyce made Bloom a Jew partly to create a sense of difference and isolation as he wanders about the city of Dublin, the proverbial wandering Jew, just as Ulysses wandered in the myth. At one time he meets racism in the form of a drunken nationalist in a pub and is roused to retort, after being called a filthy Jew, that the Republican's saviour was also a Jew. Another famous member of the Irish Jewish community – this time a real person – was Cheim Herzog, a former president of Israel.

Ireland's Muslims

Ireland has a fairly recent and fluid Muslim population of around 3,000 people. Many of them have arrived as students and spend only the period of their education in the country while others, especially some from Pakistan living in Northern Ireland, arrived as immigrants during the 1960s and 1970s. They are less homogenous than Ireland's Jews, originating from as many as thirty different countries from Malaysia to the Middle East and Pakistan to the former Yugoslavia. More settled groups live in the smaller cities and towns of Ireland working in businesses such as meat exporting factories where the meat is slaughtered according to Islamic ritual.

The Muslim community in Dublin is sufficiently large to have set up its own mosque in an abandoned Presbyterian church on the South Circular Road. The mosque has an Imam who came from the Sudan especially to take charge of the religious needs of Dublin's Muslims. The old church serves as a mosque, a social centre and a study centre. They experience little prejudice from Irish people, those with experience of Britain agreeing that it is nothing compared to the unpleasantness they have experienced there. Services in the mosque are in Arabic and English.

Other Muslims have married Irish people and somehow managed to integrate both religions' dictate that the children be brought up within their own religion. Muslim women in Ireland tend to stay at home, wearing the hajib – the face covering shawl – and mix only with the men of their family. A career is often a temporary measure before they marry and dedicate themselves to their family. They make arranged marriages and, far from feeling restricted in their own lives, they see Irish women's inability to divorce and the religious laws against contraception and abortion as denials of rights that they have and Irish women do not.

The Chinese

Surprisingly for a country with no connections in the Far East, the Chinese are the largest ethnic minority in Ireland. In the Republic it is thought that there are about 5,000 legal Chinese residents, whether Irish citizens, European Union citizens or working in Ireland on a work permit. There are many more if the illegal immigrants are added. In line with the stereotype many of the Irish Chinese actually do work in the catering industry in small takeaway restaurants as well as larger, more exclusive places.

Chinese people have a long tradition of hard work and very little concept of the welfare state. Ireland has for many Chinese people been the perfect place to set up in business. Until recent years there was little competition in the catering industry and in the major cities Chinese takeaways and restaurants are as Irish as cabbage and potatoes. The authorities now keep a careful eye on work permits being sought for people in catering, encouraging Chinese restaurateurs to employ Irish people rather than foreign Chinese.

In Northern Ireland, Chinese is the most widely spoken language after English. There are about 8,000 ethnic Chinese in Northern Ireland. The Chinese community in Belfast is quite close and, being recent, even experiences language problems. Most Chinese people in Belfast and the North in general are from Hong Kong. Just as the Irish in New York or London stay in a close knit group using certain pubs and social clubs so do the Chinese, organising karaoke nights and showings of Hong Kong movies.

Just as in the south, only more so, the Chinese are associated with the catering trade, the first generation immigrants running Chinese takeaways, working enormously long hours and communicating with their Catholic or Protestant neighbours only in the words of their

menus. Chinese restaurants tend to get most of their business after the pubs close so working hours are unsocial to say the least. Many Chinese women in particular do not learn English readily and, apart from their family and Chinese friends, lead fairly isolated lives. They exist outside the conflict of the rest of Belfast having establishments in both the Falls and Shankill roads – the Catholic and Protestant strongholds – and throughout the city. They can often walk from one sectarian area to another where other residents would hesitate, with good reason. Their children tend to go to schools where there are other Chinese students. One school of 400 pupils has 22 Chinese students.

Socially, young Chinese people do not mix very much with their Northern Ireland peers. Cities like Belfast and Derry can be scary places at night and dance clubs are often sectarian in nature. The complexities of the political situation are probably lost on a community of people used to gang warfare among rival groups in Hong Kong. Many Chinese people who arrived in Northern Ireland before the Troubles really began left during the worst of the fighting. As things have calmed down in the late 1980s and 1990s many have returned and found the burgeoning nightlife of Belfast and Derry perfect ground for re-establishing business. Many have gone from strength to strength, opening more luxurious places, catering to more gourmet inclined clientele, or other shops where the working hours are less demanding.

Indians

A small number of people from India have settled in both the Republic and Northern Ireland, beginning in the late 1940s. There are about a thousand Indians, mostly Hindus, living in the North and probably around two thousand ethnic Indians in the Republic, although figures do not distinguish between India and Pakistan and European Union citizens would not register in the figures anyway. Generally speaking they arrived with a good education and money or came with the purpose of education or setting up a business.

Among the people who have made a new home for themselves in Ireland many have set up small enterprises making a simple living.

Like their British peers, many of the young Indians in Belfast or Dublin have distinct local accents and have learned Irish in school if they are from the Republic. Their areas of work are sometimes in catering, in the Indian takeaways and the very few upmarket Indian restaurants around the country, but they figure more largely in industries such as electronics or small businesses such as dry cleaning. There are many Indian doctors in Ireland. A recent survey in the North showed that Indians were responsible for the creation of about 3,000 jobs, a figure well respected in a country with around 20% unemployment. The president of Belfast's Chamber of Trade is Diljit Rana, who came to Ireland in 1967 with a good education but little else and now owns a major new hotel, restaurants and other business enterprises. Indian children are generally successful in school and the community experiences little of the prejudice so common in Britain.

The Japanese

About 500 Japanese management executives live in Ireland at any one time, mostly on short term contracts setting up businesses for Japanese firms. They are issued with work permits because they bring the expertise of the firm with them which cannot be reproduced by an Irish or European Union citizen. The executives tend to stay for two or three years and bring their families with them. This can cause problems for the children whose school regime would be much more relaxed in Ireland than the very competitive system that operates in Japan. Many of them attend the Sudai International School in Kildare where they can keep up with the demands of the Japanese school system. Those who attend regular schools tend to rely heavily on private tuition and weekend classes. Older students are far more likely to remain in Japan for their higher education. In order to make their temporary stay in Ireland more settled, Japanese firms have set up a Japan Friendly Society, which gives courses on Irish culture and ways to integrate with Irish neighbours. For many Japanese people the easy going, light hearted Irish must seem a peculiar group of people.

Europeans

Over the years many Europeans have settled in Ireland for many reasons. During the 1960s when property prices were low in Ireland and fears about nuclear accidents were growing, many Germans and French bought little cottages all over Ireland and prepared them for their retirement. The number of Europeans entering what was then not part of the European Union began to cause alarm to the point where one Teach Dáil raised the issue in the Dáil, asking if it were right with so many Irish people leaving the countryside for the cities that foreigners should be allowed to take up all the old houses.

The move from Europe to Ireland has been steady if not overwhelming. European small business operators get tax concessions and low rents for setting up businesses that employ a certain number of Irish people. Ireland is one of the few really unspoiled countries left in a highly polluted and overpopulated continent and the beauty of its countryside and the easy going nature of the local people attract many first time visitors to stay. All over the west of Ireland tiny businesses are run by Europeans – budget hostels, restaurants, organic farms, goat rearing, craft shops, even small engineering firms and furniture manufacturers. In any small town in the west of Ireland on Fair-day or just on Fridays, when all the shopping gets done, you are as likely to hear French or German spoken as English.

It is important to point out to the aspiring Gaelophile that Ireland's Europeans fall into two distinct categories – labelled 'blow-ins' and 'hippies' (yes, hippies!) in some parts of the country. Blow-ins are the respectable looking ones who wear wax jackets and sensible shoes and drive small, ecologically sound, four-wheel-drive cars with Greenpeace stickers in the windows. Hippies, on the other hand, have unusual hair styles (pony tails or rats tails if they are men and shaved bits if they are women), Oxfam shop clothes, especially overcoats and woollen jumpers with holes in them and Doc Marten boots. The men carry shoulder bags (to keep their dope in according to the locals) and the women have multiple pierced ears. Babies are dressed in colourful scarves, hand knitted items made from scraps of wool and have dreadlock hairstyles. Hippy vehicles are usually camper-vans, are uniformly old and artily painted like the original hippy carriages of the 1960s. Blow-ins are often affluent, are older and, if they work at all, run small businesses such as cafeterias or herb farms.

RELIGIOUS ETHNICITY

The one division in Ireland that the whole world must be aware of is that of religion. In Northern Ireland the division has been almost complete with few Protestant and Catholic families mixing or having much idea of the lives of their close neighbours until the relative easing of tensions in the 1990s. Nowadays, in cities like Belfast, younger people mix a little in places like stand-up comedy bars where religious divisions can often be a source of humour between the performers and their audience. Queens University in Belfast is probably one of the first places where young Northerners meet people of the other religion.

In social terms the lives of these two divided peoples are remarkably similar. They watch the same television programmes, have the same aspirations for their children, worship the same god and equally suffer the worst of the strife. They have more in common with each other than with their English compatriots, both groups professing religious belief in higher numbers and attending church far more regularly than the English. But anyone in the North can be identified by their fellow citizens as Protestant or Catholic within minutes of finding out what school they attend or what area they live in and, in many cases, by what job they do.

CLASS DIVISIONS

Similarly the typical British division of class does not apply. In Britain listening to someone speak tells a great deal about their social origins, expectations, even their earning power. In Ireland class does not reveal itself in this manner. A rich farmer is still a culchie and a posh Dublin 4 speaker is still a jackeen.

The more significant difference between social groups in Ireland is the division between country and city, particularly the difference between Dublin and the rest of Ireland. Although it is a small city by European standards Dublin has many of the attributes of city life, from sprawling suburbs to badly planned 1960s housing estates driven by poverty, violence and street crime. It also has a lively and creative social scene with avant-garde theatre, concerts, all the movies the rest of Europe is watching, shopping centres, traffic jams, industrial estates, ring roads and a metro system called the DART.

A typical country town, say Skibbereen in County Cork, has a few blocks of houses and shops, one or maybe two functioning supermarkets, lots of small shops of the kind that disappeared from the rest of Europe a decade ago, such as a saddlers or drapers, lots of pubs, possibly a cinema and about three blocks of street lights and pavements. Beyond that houses mingle with warehouses and small businesses and finally give way to small stone walled fields with small herds of cows or the occasional flock of sheep. The town will serve as a centre for the many tiny villages that break up the pattern of fields. Each village will have a church, perhaps a post office and school and maybe a creamery and small shop and of course at least two pubs.

Most people in the country rarely walk anywhere if they can drive and it is not unusual to find the road blocked by two farmers exchanging the time of day, one in either lane of the two lane roads that are typical of rural Ireland. Driving through rural Ireland it is still common practise, at least in some parts, to give a wave to anyone seen walking on the road. If you walk past someone also walking your chances of not engaging in several minutes of chat are very low. This is not the case in Dublin where they would think you mad if you said hello to everyone you passed in the street. Many people walking along the roads in the country will also expect a lift to the nearest town unless your car is full. A similar offer in the city might get you arrested. When you do offer lifts you can expect to be questioned about your origins, Irish connections, length of stay and job prospects. In the small towns of rural Ireland everyone knows everyone else. I recently needed to contact the mother of one of my son's friends. We didn't know her first name or address but knew she was a headmistress. I asked in one of the two town newsagents and got the address, phone number and some bio-data within about two minutes. In the smaller cities this might still be possible to a limited extent but, like European cities, Dublin can be quite anonymous.

Life is different in many other ways between the city and the country. There are far fewer amenities or services in the country but there is lots of fresh air and some truly beautiful scenery. This slower pace, more restricted outlook and the quality of the surroundings breeds a different kind of person. The city people call the country people culchies as a term of abuse. It means that they have little experience of city things like escalators or self service petrol stations and so lack the sophistication of their city relatives. In turn the small town people call the farmers culchies meaning that they have no familiarity with town things like cash dispensers and traffic lights or the cinema. Even voting patterns can be distinguished between the country and the city. In the cities the old distinctions between Fianna Fail and Fine Gael have gone and people vote for parties like the Labour Party or the Progressive Democrats. In the country people vote according to who they owe a favour to or more likely which party their great grandparents supported during the Civil War. In the cities the popular ideas in America or Europe about tracing one's roots have not yet caught hold. Too many of the city folk are newly urbanised and any reminder of their rural past, beyond the occasional visit to the family farm, is unwelcome. Very few people would consider return- ing to the country to live.

The Anglo-Irish

After the Partition in 1920 the numbers of Protestant people in the Republic fell away sharply either through emigration or intermar- riage. Remaining in tiny numbers and ageing fast are some wonderful relics of a bygone age – the Anglo-Irish. Despite the fact that they, like their parents and their grandparents, have lived in Ireland they speak with English accents that would normally be heard in the bourgeois counties of England's south coast. They live in ancient crumbling old houses, for the most part as elderly as they are, drive cars they inherited from their parents and generally live a lifestyle that ended for the rest of Ireland fifty years ago.

An excellent way to see this rare and endangered species is to attend a local concert of classical music. These are often organised by local choral societies and often take place in Church of Ireland churches. The Anglo-Irish can be distinguished by their loud imperious voices, ancient fox furs or hacking jackets and cravats. They really are a rare and wonderful sight and one has to admire whatever sense of belonging or endurance has kept them in a society which has long since stopped touching its forelock to them. A friend of mine once stopped his car to help an elderly Anglo-Irish lady and her elderly car which had a flat tyre. He jacked up the car, took off the tyre and replaced it with the spare, all the time thinking he was kindly helping out an elderly lady. When he had finished she gave him 50p as a gratuity. Not only was that insulting it was also too little!

Chapter Thirteen

A DAY AT THE RACES

Beauing, belleing, dancing, drinking,
Breaking windows, damning,
Ever raking, never thinking,
Live the rakes of mallow.
　　　　—*The Rakes of Mallow*
　　　　　　Nineteenth century song

THE IRISH LEISURE ETHIC

If Ireland has few of the megabuck leisure centres of other European countries that doesn't mean the Irish don't know how to enjoy themselves. An adventure park like Alton Towers in Britain or Ocean Park in Hong Kong would certainly attract a lot of visitors among the Irish but home grown leisure pursuits are just as entertaining. The day to day leisure activity of most people is of course the pub and it could be quite difficult to live in Ireland for any length of time unless you were happy to spend your nights drinking with friends.

Another leisure pursuit for most Irish people is talking about their neighbours, or national identities. Even the British Royal Family gets aired regularly, especially when one of them does something gossip-worthy. Mary Robinson's skirt length is another topic with which people while away a few minutes and of course the weather can take up whole hours. Ireland is a country which is peculiarly susceptible to the changes in the weather and for the 50% of the population who live in the countryside it is constantly on their mind. The weather of course can also affect other leisure pursuits besides chat.

Racing

One of Ireland's many semi-nationalised industries is bloodstock. Horse breeding and racing and betting on the races is a serious business as well as a perfect opportunity for a party. In fact Ireland invented the steeplechase when, in 1752, a Mr Blake bet Mr O'Callaghan that he could race him from the church steeple of Buttevant in their home county of Cork to a neighbouring steeple, four and a half miles away. The two riders took whatever route they chose, jumping over whatever walls and ditches got in the way. History does not record which of them won but the race caught on and is probably the most loved and widely followed type of racing in Ireland, even if it is not the most lucrative. Steeplechasers are geldings so no matter how successful they are they can only win prize money and whatever bets their owners place on the race.

Like children everywhere these Irish boys take their fun where they find it.

The real money in Irish racing is in the horses that take part in flat racing, a shorter, faster race on a flat surface, either dirt or grass. Successful flat racing horses may go on after their day is done to bring in millions of pounds for the country in breeding. Hundreds of mares from all over Europe and beyond are brought to Ireland annually to be bred and the profits from the services are tax free to the bloodstock owner. Ireland earns about I£65 million a year in exports from the bloodstock industry. 12,000 people work in the horse racing industry generally and there are 348 registered trainers and 7,000 registered breeders of thoroughbred racehorces.

Industry aside, horse racing is a major social activity in Ireland and it is largely free from the kind of snobbery and class consciousness of its British counterpart. Over a million people go to the 269 various horse meetings scattered throughout the year. The biggest must be the

Irish Grand National held on Easter Monday each year at Fairyhouse in County Dublin. Other big events are The Punchestown Festival in March and the Irish Derby in June. Total betting on all Irish races is around I£103 million a year. Besides these big events different groups have their favourite racing festivals, the most popular one being Listowel in the Autumn. This race is held at the time when farmers have finished with the year's work and are ready to spend a bit of cash.

The races at Killarney in May are a kind of start up to the tourist season and are really aimed at those horse lovers who are also drink lovers – it is far less of a race meet and more of a good booze-up. From Killarney the dedicated horse lovers can move on right around the country from one festival meet to another. These festivals are only partly horse racing events. They are also good places to buy and sell a horse, not necessarily racehorses but horses of a more workaday manner. Good food, music and drink accompany all of them and all the local bars get week long extensions to their licences so drinking goes on well into the early hours. One particularly interesting meet is at Listowel in County Kerry, where the race track is the beach and the race buildings consist of the nearby public toilets. The starting time of the race is determined by the tides, since the track is covered by water at high tide. Huge marquees are erected in the field behind the beach where the horses parade before the race. Local huntsmen police the beach, keeping sand-castle building children off the racetrack. Few of the big names in racing go to the race but many keener people with more to play for, such as making a name in the sport, attend.

The centre for flat racing is the Curragh where the various prize monies range around the I£50,000 to the I£150,000 mark. Most of the big bloodstock farms are around this area too. At the flat races there is perhaps a more serious air to things with horse owners looking for good breeding stock and much wheeler-dealing taking place. Designer wear and hats are also more common at the Curragh races. Some of the world's biggest and most well known horses came from Ireland – Red Rum, three times winner of the British Grand National,

Shergar, the victim of an IRA abduction, Nijinsky, and of course Arkle, whose bones are on display at the national Stud in Kildare.

Horses are still well loved animals among the Irish. Twenty years ago horses were still used in the fields of Ireland and many of them are kept by local small farmers just for the pleasure of having the animals at hand. All over the west of Ireland tiny local horse races are still arranged like the one at Durrus, a tiny village in County Cork, every St. Stephen's day, when local people bring out their ponies for a race through the village's single street. The Travellers still breed and trade horses and many small farmers still have their old ploughs, even if they are only brought out for ploughing competitions or during the tourist season.

Going to the Dogs

If horse racing has taken on a more classy image in the days since farmers met to show off and race their horses in local fields then greyhound racing is the more proletarian activity in the cites of Ireland.

It is a very young sport in Ireland compared to horse racing. The first dog race in Ireland was in 1927 in Belfast. There are eighteen tracks around the country, eight of them owned by a semi-state company. Betting comes to around I£33 million a year and tracks are attended by about three quarters of a million people annually. A breeding stock of Irish greyhounds is being developed but so far Irish greyhounds have not yet acquired the status of Irish horses. Dog racing in Ireland is still a man's activity though, with open stands and few facilities.

Hare coursing is another, more controversial Irish leisure activity, with the dogs in this case chasing live hares. In 1993 legislation was passed requiring that the dogs be muzzled and the hare inspected for injury after the event, so hopefully much of the gore has gone out of this particular activity.

Boxing

Another popular sport in Ireland recently has been boxing, after the success in the 1992 Olympic Games of Michael Carruth and Wayne McCullagh, although boxing is poorly funded and a very working class, male sport. The Irish Amateur Boxing Association covers the whole island and it was particularly sad when the two men came back to Ireland and a huge public welcome was given to both the Dubliner and the Belfast man in Dublin but only McCullagh received any official public acclaim in Belfast. A good number of young men are involved in boxing in the Republic and its council estate image is due to the fact that many of the men who organise and run the clubs do so as a means of keeping potential delinquents off the streets. Very few of the youngsters go on to senior level which is practised in a small way in the universities and the army. Carruth was, and still is, a sergeant in the Irish Army.

SPORT AND POLITICS: THE GAA

The Gaelic Athletic Association (GAA) was founded in 1884 as part of the Gaelic revival of that period. At the time sport was dominated by the wealthy Anglo-Irish class and consisted largely of English sports such as cricket and rugby. In addition sport was prohibited on Sundays, the only day when the Catholic poor had the leisure time to play any sport. In fact *Lawrence's Handbook of Cricket in Ireland*, a manual of sporting rules, excluded any mechanics, artisans or labourers from taking part in gentleman's amateur athletics.

The GAA was set up to re-establish the ancient Irish sports and perhaps invent a few new ones. Sport, nationalism and religion became fused together as nationalists took up sports to show their nationalism and sportsmen took up nationalism as part of their interest in sport. The GAA set out rules for the traditional sports of Gaelic football, hurling and camogie, the women's version of hurling. The British armed forces and the British police were banned from playing and anyone who played other games besides the traditional Irish ones were also banned. The ban on other competitors taking part was lifted in 1971 but the ban on Royal Ulster Constabulary policemen and servicemen taking part is still in place, although it is unlikely that many want to take part. Unluckily one GAA ground happened to be right on the border in County Armagh when the Partition took place. It was confiscated and is still occupied by British troops.

The GAA became immensely popular all over Ireland and still is. It no doubt prevented the ultimate loss of traditional Irish games from Irish life but despite its good intentions it has become another area of discord between Republicans and Protestants. The GAA was listed by Protestant paramilitaries as a legitimate target for bombing. It is sectarian in nature and as recently as 1991 behaved badly over a planned Gaelic football and English football event to be held in the GAA grounds in Croke Park, Dublin. Using an obscure rule about sharing profits with non-GAA sports it called the festival off and brought severe criticism down on itself from all parties, including the gentle Mary Robinson. In recent years the whole issue has become more fraught than ever as a Northern Irish Gaelic football team, Derry, has taken part for the last three years in the finals of the All Ireland Football League. The games have been screened by the BBC and watched by a quarter of a million people and the Ulster Unionist groups see this coverage as part of British attempts to quietly reintroduce a sense of Irish unity.

GAA members in the North have been targeted by Protestant paramilitary groups and there have been firebomb attacks on clubhouses. For their part the GAA claim that they are harassed by the security forces with helicopters buzzing matches and armed soldiers pointing their weapons at the crowds during matches. Gaelic football is the most popular of the Irish sports and is a kind of cross between American football and British rugby. It is an extremely physical game and moves at a very fast pace, making it a very exciting and spectacular sport for the spectator.

Hurling

All this is a long way from what sport is to most people in the world. Still, Irish sports are a grand affair to watch, hurling being a kind of violent hockey with raised sticks and protective headgear. Camogie is played only by women and is a gentler form of hurling. There are three forms of hurling games played at the *Poc Fada Na h'Eireann* Festival at Limerick. The team game is 2,000 years old and was once called *baire baoise* or imitation warfare. Teams were originally 21 strong and games were played until one team remained alive. At the Battle of Moytura the real war was preceded by a game of hurling in which 400 people are said to have died. The Poc Fada has been recently revived although no-one dies any more. The Poc Fada

commemorates the day, lost in myth, when Sedanta, a folk hero, slayed a hound that guarded the land of Culann the Smith by hurling a stone down its throat. This gave him the new name Cu Chullain and he took over the job of guarding the land with his hurling bat.

In the other two hurling games played at the Poc Fada Festival competitors test their strength and accuracy with three hurling shots at a fixed target which is in the form of a hound's head. In the more traditional game competitors hit the hurling ball, or *sliothar*, over a mountain course about three miles long. The aim is to cover the ground in as few shots as possible. The hurl is achieved by balancing the ball on the stick, raising it above the shoulder and propelling it skywards. A referee chases the ball and marks its landing spot from where the next hurl is made. The sport is watched by many a hardy spectator, sitting out on the mountainside covered in blankets and ducking the hurling balls. The players are sponsored by local firms and the bagpipes are out for the occasion.

Perhaps because of the national interest in football, hurling is rapidly losing players and support. It is an expensive game to organise and although there are subsidies available to maintain the county hurling teams not all of the available cash is claimed. Hurling is no longer taught in all the schools in Ireland, only around a third of all primary schools and fewer secondary schools now teach it.

Road Bowling

An even more esoteric activity than hurling leather balls across mountains takes place in only two areas of Ireland and is unknown anywhere else. Road bowling is to the people of West Cork and County Antrim what basketball or baseball is to many Americans. The game is ludicrously simple and surely must be related to the hurling game from Limerick. The game is an individual sport with any number of men taking part in the competition.

In road bowling a section of road is marked out, start and finish lines are painted on and the game begins. Since the game has to be played on the public road it is only ever played on Sundays and along the very tiny roads of the Irish countryside. A big straight European dual carriageway would defeat the object of the game, which is to get the ball, by whatever route, from one point to the other in the least number of throws. If the road goes round a bend it is legitimate to try and throw the ball across the bend, thus cutting out a few yards. Unlike the leather hurling ball, the ball used in this game is made of steel and weighs 28 ounces. Your first and only sight of one of these games will be coming across a group of men and boys standing at the side of the road as you drive through the back lanes on Sunday afternoon. People often travel a long way to take part in a bowling match and a great deal of betting goes on, especially when two famous bowlers meet one another. Inter-county games often take place with teams from Antrim visiting Cork or vice versa. A good bowler is not necessarily the strongest man. Quite small men have won bowling matches. The skill is in judging the road and finding ways to cut corners rather than strength in throwing.

Fishing

One of Ireland's major attractions to tourists has always been the excellent fishing, whether sea fishing or fishing the inland waterways. Many of the best trout streams were carefully incorporated into the local lord's estates in the years of the Anglo-Irish ascendancy and are still privately owned and carefully guarded where the owners can make a great deal of money from fishing tourism. But there are still many waterways with salmon and trout available to the everyday angler and Irish people have taken to the sport in greater numbers in recent years. For some reason the sport appeals to many teenagers who are happy to wander off for a day sitting by the side of a lake or river hoping for a trout or two.

The Fisheries Board now stocks many lakes with rainbow trout which are not indigenous fish and do not breed in the lakes. The natural fish of the inland lakes and mountain streams is the brown trout which never gets very big and is bottom of the fisherman's list. Where lakes feed down to the sea through unpolluted and undisturbed rivers there are salmon trout which live for most of the year in the sea but swim ashore to breed and lay eggs as far up the river of their choice as they can. These fish are the best of the Irish catch and high prices are paid for them by restaurants. Fishing for them is restricted to certain months of the year when least damage to the egg laying females is done. Each salmon always returns to the same river from which it emerged as a fry, and swims up it, against what is often a strong current, to the spawning grounds. The salmon are at their best at the very mouth of the river before all their stored energy is expended in the long journey upstream. As they return downstream they are less of a catch but still worthwhile.

Fishing off the rocks in Bantry Bay – a restful pursuit with the added bonus of bringing home your dinner.

Many tourists come to Ireland just for the fishing. Ireland's waterways are the purest in Europe and there are many rivers where salmon can be caught and the tranquil beauty of Ireland's river systems can be enjoyed. There are of course quite a few fishing festivals all over the island and the dedicated angler, like the dedicated race-goer, can spend the best part of the summer and autumn going from one festival to another, competing in the various competitions and boasting about the one that got away at night, while listening to the usual crack and music in the local pubs, which will no doubt keep serving until the tall tales have all been told.

Sea fishing is another roaring trade in the summer, as tourists can go out after many of the big fish, such as shark, that cruise the waters of Ireland. This gets a little more expensive than fresh water fishing and is less popular as a pastime among local people. It is more likely that an Irish person with a small boat will use it to supplement their income, catching scallops or mackerel to sell locally. Many more people fish from the shore all around Ireland's coastline where flounder, pollack, mackerel, ray and many other table fish can be caught.

Seaside Recreation

The sea is the chief occupation of a very small number of Irish people considering the huge coastline and safe harbours but it attracts a lot of sea sports fanatics from small yacht owners to surfers, windsurfers, dolphin watchers and swimmers. At weekends and the traditional holiday weeks in July the beaches fill up with families sunbathing, buying hotdogs from vans parked nearby, playing ball games, building sand-castles and generally getting sand in everything.

Ireland has some exquisite beaches which are almost mind bogglingly clean, empty and undeveloped compared to the beaches of the Costa Brava or the south coast of England. Ireland doesn't have the weather of the Costa Brava either, so it is unlikely that they will ever become like the beaches of warmer European climates.

In life we are death. Enjoying a day at the beach while the ancestors look out over Bantry Bay.

One seaside town that approaches the more usual holiday resort of the rest of Europe is Bundoran in County Donegal, which is close to the urban areas of Northern Ireland. In summer lots of Catholic families take their holidays there and stay in the hotels or caravan parks of the area. The town's main street is full of amusement arcades dating back, in some cases, to the sixties with penny rolling games alongside the computer games of the nineties. At night the pubs are full of men singing rebel songs and, until recently, English accented visitors may have been advised to leave.

Ireland's weather is not conducive to the types of activities that are normally associated with a beach holiday but it does have some very spectacular coastline scenery. The western side of the island is exposed to the Atlantic Ocean and this has, over the ages, led to the formation of some wonderfully rugged and imposing shoreline. A trip to the coast or even a visit to a seaside resort town like Bundoran can certainly be a rich, and uniquely Irish, experience.

Fife and Drum Bands

In Northern Ireland the old traditions are still kept up by nationalist and unionist diehards and one of these is the Protestant fife and drum band. The bands are entirely sectarian in nature and their purpose is political rather than cultural. The bands practise all year for the celebration of the Battle of the Boyne on July 12. On that day they parade around the city streets in uniform playing Unionist tunes on the huge lambeg drum and the flute-like fifes. For their part the nationalist youths play pipes and they too wear uniforms and march on the twelfth, not to celebrate the success of the Orange troops but to assert their nationalism. In the past, Protestant marching bands would march through the districts dominated by the other side and often provoke running battles between the two groups.

Soccer

As in so may other things the North and the Republic are divided by football. Northern Ireland has had a quite successful international soccer team for many years, its star player of all time being George Best, whose reputation as a carouser and drinker overshadows his legendary skill as a footballer. In recent years football has become more popular in the Republic with the national team being managed by Jackie Charlton, who has no Irish connections, but who has taken the team and given it international status. He has made use of a regulation which allows any English person of Irish descent to play in the Irish team and now has many English team players on the side.

In the 1990 World Cup in Italy the Irish team astounded even themselves by getting as far as the quarter-finals and Ireland painted itself green and orange and watched television for the summer as the Irish team went from strength to strength. Ireland qualified again for the 1994 World Cup in the United States, much to the delight of the fans, but after a good start the Irish team failed to get into the quarter finals, disappointing thousands of people, who nevertheless gave them a heroes' welcome on their return.

In 1993 the Irish team played Northern Ireland in Belfast and security was very high. The game was important to the Republic who needed a win to qualify for the World Cup but the Northern Ireland team had already failed to qualify. Republic supporters were advised not to travel north to support their team and few did. There were no serious incidents but Northern Ireland fans were disappointed when The Republic scored one goal, winning the match.

Jackie Charlton, the manager of the Republic's national team, was one of the members of the English 1966 winning World Cup team and is a great character. He is liked by all Irish people despite his tendency for plain speaking and was recently given the freedom of the city of Dublin. He has entered into Irish social life with enthusiasm and is often to be seen on television chat shows or hosting a popular programme about fishing, another of his interests.

The Republic has a professional football league with about twelve teams competing. It is less popular than soccer in Britain since it faces competition from Gaelic football but is growing in support all the time with the success of the national team.

The Open Road

If driving isn't a national leisure activity in Ireland it is surely a national pastime. No-one with a car walks anywhere if they can help it and a common sight in the country is to see a farmer literally driving his cows into the milking shed. The cows walk at their usual leisurely pace with the farmer in first gear gently edging them along and swerving around to keep stragglers in line. Cars are not the status symbol in Ireland that they are in many other countries and if someone has a very new or flashy car they are likely to be subjected to a degree of slagging for it.

Cars in a particularly bad sate can be stopped and tested for roadworthiness if the police are so inclined and Irish cars, especially in the countryside, achieve new heights of decay unknown anywhere else in the western world. It is not an uncommon sight for a car to be held together with bits of baling wire, especially on some of the offshore islands where a good day's fun can be had spotting the rustiest car. The climate can add to the degree and quality of rust in cars that are rarely kept in a garage and sit out in the worst of the winter weather. They are also used for many different jobs around the farm and are often full of bits of straw or farm machinery and occasionally livestock.

Driving too is a characteristically Irish piece of behaviour with individuals being well known for their peculiar habits, like driving in second gear only, or stopping in the middle of the road to chat to friends. Newcomers to the island should be warned about driving and Irish roads. Out of the big cities most roads are two lane affairs often with heavy vehicles on them which can create long tailbacks. The roads are also likely to have herds of cows wandering about them or, where I live, even donkeys. Tractors with bales of hay doing about ten miles an hour are a common sight and although many will pull over to let visitors pass they can slow a journey no end. Ireland is also ill-prepared for icy weather since it occurs so rarely and in the few spells of snow that occur roads simply close for the duration.

— Chapter Fourteen —

D.I.Y. IRELAND

When the soul of a man is born in this country there are nets flung at it to hold it back from flight. You talk to me of nationality, language, religion. I shall try to fly by those nets.

—James Joyce
A Portrait of the Artist as a Young Man

THE FINER POINTS

This chapter is a kind of quick reference guide to all things Irish not covered in the other chapters. With their keen sense of history and long memories the Irish tend to speak within a context which goes back many years and can be slightly confusing to those who know little of the ins and outs of Irish life.

Greetings

The Irish are pretty much a 'take us as you meet us' people. There are few courtesies which are peculiar to the Irish but a few points should be mentioned. In Ireland you might find yourself required to spend more time over greetings than you are used to. Most people like a conversation to begin with a greeting, whether you are dealing with a shop assistant or someone you are asking directions of, or even people you pass on the road in less populated areas.

When meeting strangers in Ireland, on however casual a basis, expect a few pertinent enquiries about matters like your origins, work and destination. Irish people like to have a whole picture of the person they are dealing with and like to pass that on to their neighbours. A handshake is a common form of greeting between both men and women but embracing is rare – except among urban yuppies – and not at all between men and women. In the countryside make sure you are not moving into the person's private space. Most country people spend a lot of time in the open and expect a wider distance to be kept between you and them than city people. If you are female you might want to prepare to smile understandingly at an assumed male superiority. Male condescension isn't intended to insult, it's rather the result of years of paternalism.

In pubs you will be greeted on entry unless the place is heaving and will also be thanked and bid goodbye on leaving. Goodbyes are probably more widely used than in other contexts. You would bid the shop assistant good luck or goodbye when leaving. Look out for some interesting body language in this context. A barely noticeable flick of the head can often mean goodbye. 'God bless' is another regularly used farewell. Irish people would accept whatever form of salutation you choose to use but try to avoid patronising terms like, 'top of the morning to you' – this is pure stage Irish and is never used.

Dress

As in all things, Ireland is gradually working its way towards a European standard as regards attitudes to dress. We have already seen that people in unusual clothes or even untidy clothes get labelled hippy, particularly in the country, so if anything, dress up rather than down. That isn't to say that Irish country folk are chic but rather that they have two standards – those for themselves and those for visitors.

In any country town you will see some wonderful old suits on some wonderful old men as people often dress up to go to town. In the city casual dress is the norm and there is little power dressing among women, who do however tend to look smart when at work. As regards exposed flesh it is best to err on the side of modesty. A man won't be arrested if he walks through town with no shirt on but it won't be approved of. Similarly, short shorts on women don't go down well but no-one will take you up on it. On the beach bikinis are acceptable but you're unlikely to find topless beaches anywhere although some of the beaches around Dublin were traditionally reserved for nude male bathing. For evening wear cleavage is probably best left to the imagination although bare backs are OK.

Toilets

Back in the bad old days there were no public toilets for women in Ireland and even nowadays public toilets are elusive. Department stores and libraries cannot be relied on to have them but shopping malls do. Most people dash into the nearest pub which will usually be so full that no-one will notice you. Restaurants always have toilets so be sure you use them before you leave because you may find yourself hunting around reluctant to go into a pub without buying a drink.

Names

Irish people like to get your name and use it in conversation. First names are used more than the formal surname. In fact I have rarely been addressed by my surname in Ireland and in a business context first names are customary too. You will find that many Irish people sometimes spell their names in the Gaelic way so what may look unpronounceable – Maire or O'Suilleabhan for example – turn out to be quite familiar names (Maura, O'Sullivan). If you are addressing a priest he will be used to being called 'Father,' even by people who don't practise his religion.

Bad Language

Irish people have a peculiar attitude to swearing. Young people seem to use it as a form of punctuation or an adjective expressing degree but instead of using the usual words they change one of the vowels. The word is still recognisable but only carries a shock value for the listener who isn't used to hearing such language in everyday situations.

It is obviously better not to use bad language in company. It sounds much nastier when not pronounced in an Irish accent and it can be difficult to tell when it is acceptable or not. Generally speaking the younger, and more male, the company the bluer the language. Using the name of God seems to be quite widespread although it is frowned upon. Expressions like 'Lord save us' are common and less offensive than 'Oh my God' The expression 'Jesus, Mary and Joseph' seems to crop up a lot to express shock.

Visiting Etiquette

Generally the more 'Dublin 4' the household the more ubiquitously western the etiquette is likely to be. Home visiting isn't really very common in Ireland, where people are more likely to meet at the pub than at one another's homes. In restaurants there is far less sense of formality than in other European countries. There is a kind of sliding scale of formality in dress which correlates with the expense of the meal, although logically if you're paying a lot you ought to dress how you feel. Irish people are quite sensitive about accusations of aping the English and behaviour which suggests this is largely avoided.

Eating etiquette, however, is basically English. A formal meal would begin with soup or a starter. The next course in a meal might be fish for which strange shaped knives will be on the inside of the soup spoon. Cutlery is left tidily on the plate at the end of the course. For the main course, unless you are eating grande cuisine, the meat dish will be out in front of you on your own plate and vegetables served for the whole table. You will most likely be offered second helpings of vegetables in an Irish restaurant.

Waiters are far more casual and friendly than in other European countries and you might find yourself chatting away to them. The bill will be brought to your table at the end of the meal and tipping is pretty much expected, either handed over to the person who served your table or left on the table to be scooped up later. Whatever way you give it, the gesture will be welcomed. More expensive restaurants tend to add a 10% or 12% service charge and there is no obligation to leave any additional tip. Where you do want to tip, think in terms of 10% of the bill, or just round up the amount charged.

A warning about smoking in restaurants for nonsmokers; the most you can expect is an area reserved for nonsmokers which will be contaminated by smoke from other tables anyway. A restaurant that simply doesn't allow smoking is unusual and while you may be feeling offended because someone at a nearby table is smoking be assured that the person smoking is not conscious of any bad manners.

Weddings, Births, Deaths

Weddings are very much like they are all over the western world nowadays, with a church service followed by a reception in a local hotel. Attendance at the church is not by invitation, being a public mass anyone can attend. If you are not a Catholic and are invited to a wedding ceremony there is little to be concerned about. Worshippers tend to move between siting and standing and kneeling quite frequently but you can follow the crowd. At a stage in the mass, towards the end of the service, the congregation is invited to shake hands with one another as a sign of brotherly or sisterly love.

The reception after the mass is by invitation. People will dress up in formal clothes for weddings but it is easy to overdress. A backless evening gown or a coat and tails may go down well in a high society city wedding but generally it is simply a matter of looking smart. Lots of hats accompany suits on women, men wear their standard dark weddings and funerals suit.

The reception will consist of a meal and a party afterwards with plenty of drinks. If the party is held in a private house then all the drinks will be paid for by the wedding party. It is far more likely, however, for the celebratory party to take place in a hotel where it will undoubtedly go on well into the early hours with spontaneous recitals and Irish dancing. More food will appear during the evening. The bride and groom disappear towards the end of the party.

If you are invited to a wedding ask if there is a wedding list of suitable gifts that may be bought as presents. This is not as common as in other countries and if there isn't one then consider putting some cash (I£10-20) into an envelope and handing it over to the Best Man.

Births are relatively quiet affairs. Perhaps it's the influence of the all-male Church that lends an air of taboo to the whole act of giving birth. In the country areas the mother might be in a maternity unit miles away for a while. A visit to the baby after it has arrived home, with a small gift, is appreciated but not necessary.

Death is quite a ritualised occasion with well established procedures. When a person dies they are usually taken to a funeral home where friends may visit the body. Very few families prefer to keep the deceased at home or in the church. The coffin is accompanied by a train of sympathisers in cars as it is brought from the funeral home to the church. In a few places a wake will be held but nowadays it is little more than a formal visit to the home to pay last respects to the deceased. Close family might keep a vigil all night in the house. The clock will be stopped at the time of the person's death.

At the funeral service people wear dark colours. The family will often take part in the funeral service. The coffin is accompanied again to the cemetery with some people walking behind the coffin. A brief service at the graveside ends the formal part of the funeral. People then approach the bereaved to give their condolences and leave. For relative strangers attendance at the funeral service in the church and an appearance at the graveyard afterwards is all that is expected.

Safety

Ireland must be one of the safest places in the world in every sense of the word. First of all, there is little chance of dying from nuclear fallout unless you're on the east coast and the Sellafield nuclear reprocessing plant in the north of England blows up. Secondly, the water systems are pure and unpolluted and because there is little industry the air is remarkably clean too. Thirdly, Ireland has one of the lowest rates of death from car accidents, heart attack, and several other major killers. Suicide is high, but not the highest in Europe. Even in Northern Ireland the death rate per thousand is the lowest in the British Isles. The sexual attacks that feature in the news programmes of the rest of Europe are rarer in Ireland.

In the country in Ireland it is not unusual for cars to remain unlocked, even if parked in a public place. Car theft is very common in Dublin and not unknown in the other cities but in the countryside it is unusual for a car to be stolen and vandalism is even rarer.

Hitch-hiking is comparatively safe. Girls hitch car rides alone without too much thought for the dangers involved and people expect passing drivers to offer them a lift. In country areas the hitch-hiker will know the faces of passing motorists and a visitor should not assume that what seems a safe activity for local girls on their own is necessarily going to be the same for them. In the cities life comes closer to the European norm. You'll see burglar alarms in cars and on house walls and Dubliners have good reason to worry about muggings and car thefts.

Drug related crime is on the increase in Dublin and is beginning to spread to other urban areas. Cannabis is the most commonly available drug and from time to time great hauls of it are pulled up out of the sea off the coast of Cork and Kerry where there are innumerable small coves where small boats can slip ashore.

In the North a few precautions have to be taken in the towns and cities. Parking is a problem with designated parking areas and certain places where cars can only be left with a passenger inside. Local people will tell you if you are in one. If you leave your car in the wrong place in the North it is going to attract the attention of the security forces and if there is reason to suspect it may be carrying a bomb it may be subjected to a controlled explosion.

The good news about the North is that it all looks more intimidating than it really is. Since the Troubles erupted in 1968 not a single tourist has been killed or seriously injured as a result of political violence. And due to the heavy security presence there is far less everyday crime in places like Belfast than might be expected for a city of that size.

POLITICS

You'd need a volume just dedicated to this topic but here is a brief list of the major players and parties in the current state of affairs. The names and groupings of Northern politics is covered in the chapter on Northern Ireland.

Fianna Fail (pronounced 'fina-fall'). The party was originally formed in opposition to the treaty which created the six counties. Fianna Fail was the creation and child of Eamon De Valera, the man who masterminded the 1937 constitution and whose vision of a rural Ireland had such a lasting effect on the economy. Nowadays Fianna Fail is supported basically by people whose grandparents opposed the treaty. They have a slightly more proletarian image than their traditional opposition party, though there is nothing remotely socialist about their politics. Fianna Fail have been in power for about two thirds of the life of the Irish Republic, the last two times in coalition. Another big name in the party was Sean Lemass who headed a government in the 1950s which for the first time since the birth of the nation put some economic growth into the country and reversed the enormous tide of emigration. Recent leaders of the party include Charles Haughey and Albert Reynolds.

Fine Gael. The party that supported the treaty is now more middle class in its orientation and electorate although there is little difference between the policies of Fine Gael and Fianna Fail. Fine Gael have been in power for about one third of the time that the Republic has existed, mostly in coalition with smaller parties. Its major player of all time was Garret Fitzgerald, a man who still commands much respect in a country used to shenanigans from its political leaders. The present leader is John Bruton.

The Progressive Democrats. This party represents an odd mixture of right wing free economic doctrines and comparatively liberal policies on social issues. They are a very new party with their first few Teach Dáils taking their seats after the 1987 election. They have very few seats in the Dáil (six in 1992) but formed a coalition with Fianna Fail after the 1989 general election. They are a schism from Fianna Fail formed after Des O'Malley was expelled from the party following a critical speech in the Dáil in 1985. Des O'Malley was the man who created the party in the first place by refusing to vote against a law liberalising the law regarding contraceptives. Another key player is Mary Harney, once the youngest ever member of the upper house of the Dáil, and a minister in the 1989 Cabinet. Most of their support as a new party came from Fine Gael rather than the party they had formed a coalition government with, Fianna Fail. The alliance between the two groups was not a happy one and erupted into a slanging match in 1992 resulting in a general election.

The Labour Party. This is the oldest party in Ireland, descending from the policies of men like James Larkin, the socialist who led the Dublin lockout strike in 1913. Its leading light, James Connolly, was executed, tied to a chair, by the British after the 1916 Easter Rising.

Partly due to the politics of the Catholic Church, socialist thought has never been encouraged in Ireland and so the Labour Party has always been a minority group. But by the 1992 election, attitudes in Ireland were changing. People were getting fed up with name calling in the Dáil and tales of corruption in high places and the city vote no longer reflected traditional loyalties. The Labour Party had also softened its radical credentials and in the election won fifteen seats and formed the minority part of the cabinet in that government with Dick Spring, its leader, as Tanaiste or deputy prime minister. Mary Robinson was for a time associated with the Labour Party when she was a senator. Like the Labour Party in Britain, the Irish party no longer represents a radical alternative to the prevailing economic order.

The Democratic Left. This party was once the official IRA, a revolutionary socialist party which emerged out of the unrest of the North in the late 1960s. It went through several rightwards moves and names to eventually become the Democratic Left. It has support among the urban workers of the Republic. It got its first seat in the Dáil in the 1980s and managed to increase its numbers steadily through the

1980s, so that by 1987 there were seven Teach Dáils. They then quarrelled among themselves and the party split in 1992, losing credibility and funding. The split was over their connections with alleged criminal elements in the IRA and the party now called The Democratic Left is led by Proinsias De Rossa and is a soft left group, closer to the Labour Party than to its Sinn Féin origins.

In 1992 six of the original seven members formed the Democratic Left while the seventh, currently still in the Dáil, represents what is left of Sinn Féin, the Workers Party, which was the name it was previously known by.

Sinn Féin also contests elections in the Republic but so far has had little success. Now that peace is more likely in the North it is possible that Sinn Féin will make a greater impact in the Republic.

The Haughey Factor

This is a well known element in Irish politics or was for the years in which Charles Haughey was in government. He was a very traditional Irish leader, one whose personality and doggedness counted for more than his ideological convictions. He is the son-in-law of Sean Lemass, the influential leader of the 1950s.

During the troubles in the North he was accused and brought to trial for his alleged involvement in the buying and shipping of arms to Northern Catholics. He was acquitted but things carried on in a similar vein for most of the time he was in power.

The sources of his obvious wealth could never be explained and he became associated with various money scandals, none of which were ever actually laid at his door. He finally resigned in 1992 over phone tapping charges dating back to the 1980s. He was leader of Fianna Fail from 1979 to 1992. He spent a huge sum of government money renovating his official residence in Dublin which came to be known by local wags as the Chas (short for Charlie) Mahal.

The Albert Factor

Haughey was closely followed as leader of Fianna Fail and as Taioseach by Albert Reynolds, a one time country music promoter and dog food millionaire, known to those who love him as 'The Rhinestone Taioseach.' He precipitated the 1992 general election by calling his Tanaiste, the Progressive Democrat Des O'Malley, dishonest, followed it up by saying 'crap' on television and then twice told the country in a radio interview that his Minister for Social Welfare was trying to 'dehumanise the welfare system.' Not bad for one month's feet in the mouth!

PUBLIC HOLIDAYS AND OPENING HOURS

All over the island office hours are more or less Monday to Friday 9 am to 5 pm. What can prove to be frustrating is the custom, still common in small towns, of closing for an hour at lunch time. Post offices are open on Saturday mornings. Shops keep similar hours, often opening an hour or so later at weekends. They are closed on Sundays and usually one afternoon per week, each town having its own early closing day. On Sundays it is safe to say that Northern Ireland is closed for the day.

Pub hours are from Monday to Saturday 10 am to 11.30 pm in the Republic and during the winter, pubs close an hour earlier. In Dublin pubs close for a 'holy hour' during the afternoon. On Sundays they are open from 12.30 am to 2 pm and 4 pm to 11 pm. They are closed all day on Christmas Day and Good Friday. When a festival is on, and there are lots of them, pubs often apply for extensions which go on till one or two in the morning.

In Northern Ireland pubs are open from 11.30 am to 11 pm weekdays and Saturdays. Pubs in Protestant areas stay closed all day on Sunday. Others open from 12.30 am to 2 pm and 7 pm to 10 pm.

Public holidays sometimes differ between the Republic and Northern Ireland. Common public holidays are New Year's Day, St. Patrick's Day (March 17), Good Friday, Easter Monday, Christmas Day, and Boxing Day (December 26th is called St. Stephen's Day in the Republic). In addition the North has the first Monday in May, July 12 for the Battle of the Boyne and the last Monday in August. The Republic has May 1, the first Monday in June, the first Monday in August and the last Monday in October.

FESTIVAL CALENDAR

January	Leopardstown horse races; Naas horse races; beginning of international rugby games.
February	Dublin Film Festival; English/Irish rugby at Lansdown Park in Dublin; Belfast Music Festival.
March	St. Patrick's Day (don't expect a New York style celebration); The World Irish dancing Championships.
April	Irish Grand National, Fairyhouse, County Meath; the Gaelic football final, Croagh Park, Dublin.

May   Royal Dublin Spring Show – agricultural and farm-
              ing displays; *Fleadh Nua* – festival of traditional
              music and dance in County Clare; Cork Interna-
              tional Choral and Folk Dance Festival; Belfast
              Marathon.

June   Bloomsday, June 16 – is celebrated in Dublin with
              events of various kinds; Writer's Week Festival in
              Listowel, County Cork; The Irish Derby at the
              Curragh.

June–August Pilgrimages to Lough Derg; The Belleek Fiddle
              Stone Festival; Belfast Jazz and Blues Festival.

July   In the North Protestants take to the streets to cel-
              ebrate the Protestant victory at the Battle of the
              Boyne; fishing festivals in Athlone and County
              Mayo; pilgrimage to the summit of Croagh Patrick
              in County Mayo; Galway Arts Festival.

August   Dublin Horse Show; horse racing at Tralee, County
              Kerry; Rose of Tralee Festival, County Kerry; Puck
              Fair in the town of Killorglin, also in Kerry; Kil-
              kenny Arts Week; Connemara Pony Show; Lam-
              mas Fair in Ballycastle, County Antrim; Feile, the
              annual rock festival, in Thurles in County Tipper-
              ary during the August Bank Holiday weekend.

September   All Ireland Hurling Finals; Matchmaking Festival
              at Lisdoonvarna, County Clare; Cork Film Festival;
              Sligo Arts Week; Waterford Festival of Light Opera;
              Dublin Theatre Festival; Belfast Folk Festival.

October	Cork Jazz Festival; Dublin Theatre Festival; Dublin Marathon; Cattle and Horse Fair in Ballinasloe, County Galway; KInsale Food Festival.
November	Wexford Opera Festival; Belfast Festival.
December	Wren Boys events on St. Stephen's Day.

This list is by no means a comprehensive one. Most villages and small towns have a festival of sorts especially during the summer months.

POSTAL SERVICES AND TELEPHONES

Public phones are now modern coin or card operated machines. Phone cards are issued in denominations of 10, 20, 50 and 100 units and can be bought from post offices or shops displaying a sign. They are becoming increasingly necessary in the Republic. Call card collecting is currently an obsession with small boys and you are likely to have a pack of youngsters lurking outside the phone box, if you have an interesting high denomination card, all hoping that your card will run out and you'll leave it behind.

Making calls is as simple as it is in any other country, first dialling the international code for the country concerned and then the local digits. A five minute call locally costs around 20p. Reduced rates operate locally but for some foreign calls there is no reduced evening rate. The post office has a service where a special call card will allow you to make calls from a call box in any country charged to your home or office account. Most businesses have fax machines but these are not usually listed in the phone book.

Post offices are open from Monday to Saturday and sell stamps, as well as give out pensions and family allowances. Postage within Ireland and to the United Kingdom for a regular letter is 32p, while for abroad it starts at 52p. Letters take about 24 hours to reach their destination within Ireland and about three to five days to get to the

United Kingdom. Letters further away take a little longer. There are also courier services but much of Ireland is very rural and it is likely that if you are sending something to the west of Ireland the postal service is just as quick.

TIME

Ireland operates more or less on Greenwich mean time for most of the year. When it adjusts its time it does so in accordance with British time changes. Clocks go forward one hour in March, extending the period of daylight and go back one hour in October, reducing evening daylight. The reasons for this are lost in the mists of time but have something to do with postal workers in Britain not getting bitten by dogs in the dark. It means that from November to about February it is dark by about 4.30 in the afternoon and few children see their homes in daylight except at weekends. After December 21 the days start to draw out as 'a cock's step,' little by little, until the clocks go forward in March. From then on daylight is the norm for the whole evening until in June it is light at 11 pm in the west of Ireland. Ireland is between seven and eight hours behind the Far East and six hours ahead of the east coast of America.

MEASURES

Electricity is the same as in the United Kingdom – 220 volts AC, 50 cycles. Plugs are earthed and have three square pins. For two pin gadgets a plastic adaptor can be bought from your home country which will fit into the earth pin hole. If you have Japanese gadgets with three thin pins set at angles on the plug you will need to change the plugs or bring a special adaptor with you. Bathrooms often have two pin, 110 volt sockets for shavers and are labelled 'shavers only.'

As regards weights and measures, Ireland operates the belt and braces policy. Food shops give weights in both metric and imperial measures. Petrol is bought by the litre and beer by the pint or half pint. If you are measuring something to buy wood or cloth take the measurements in both. Some shops sell by the metre and some by feet and inches and there is no way of knowing which till you get there. The fun begins when you need to convert square feet to square metres. If you are used to the metric system and pounds and ounces confuse you, remember that one kilogram is slightly over two pounds, a litre is two and a bit pints and a metre is roughly the same as a yard.

GEOGRAPHY

Ireland is the most western part of the continent of Europe and is separated from the Continent by Britain, the English Channel and the Irish Sea. It consists of a central low lying plain surrounded by quite low mountain ranges. To the west these mountain ranges are picturesque to say the least and are a major source of income from tourism. The highest mountain is Carrantuohill in County Kerry at 1041 metres. Ireland has a maritime climate, which means it rains a lot, with a mean annual temperature of 10°C and very little frost or snow during the winter months. Summers are mild (and often intermittently wet) with an average temperature of about 17°C all

OBSERVATORY

TRIGG

thanks to the Atlantic Ocean which warms the air and dumps gallons of water, particularly around the higher mountains in the west. Some areas get as much as 270 days of rain per year. If Eskimos have lots of words for snow, then the Irish have lots of words for rain, some of them unprintable.

The River Shannon is the longest in the British Isles at 259 kilometres. Politically the island is divided into 32 counties, 26 of them in the Republic and six in Northern Ireland. Bear in mind though that when talking about northern and southern regions of Ireland there are southern or Republican counties, such as Donegal, which are further north than Northern Ireland.

The island is 84,404 square kilometres, 500 kilometres from north to south and 300 kilometres east to west. It has 5,630 kilometres of coastline. A really special place to visit geographically speaking is the Burren in County Clare which is bare limestone rock, undercut with hundreds of channels and underground caves, with a fascinating flora mixing both Mediterranean species and alpine plants.

Ireland has a resident population of about five million with millions more scattered around the rest of the world. 3.5 million live in the Republic and 1.5 million in Northern Ireland. The largest city on the island is Dublin with about 1.5 million residents. The next is Belfast with about 300,000 residents, then Cork with 175,000 followed by Limerick, Derry and Galway.

IRISH TELEVISION

Other chapters have dealt with the history and politics of Irish television. Basically most Irish people watch English television, either Ulster television if they are in the North or regular English stations if they have access to one of the relay systems which now broadcast all over Ireland. For a long time the legality of these broadcast stations was in dispute but it seems settled now. This means that most Irish people can get four British channels, two Irish channels and Sky Television channels on cable or by satellite.

Sky Television offers a package of channels with two sports channels and four movie channels. There are innumerable old American, English and Australian soaps and comedy shows. The Astra satellite also broadcasts CNN, the American news channel, and Sky News. Sky News is full of 'human interest' items, shorthand for 'news' about the royal family and details of nasty murders and so on. The movie channels get movies after they've been released on video for a while and then flog them to death for about six months before finally taking them off their schedules.

The two Irish channels do some Gaelic chat shows and news features, a couple of desperate but well loved soaps called "Fair City" and "Glenroe," some quiz games, documentaries and concert shows, two massively popular chat shows, ("The Late Late Show" and "Kenny Live") and a bunch of other locally produced material. They top this up with mostly wholesome American and English situation comedies.

Some Personalities

Dr Anthony Clare. Well known on both sides of the Irish Sea for his radio programmes in which he examines the psyches of prominent people. Dr Clare is frequently on Irish chat shows and writes on contemporary issues in the newspapers. During the debate in 1993 over a woman's right to obtain information about abortions in Britain he felt obliged to write in *The Irish Times*; "The whole notion of holding a referendum on women's access to information is such a profound disgrace for a nation such as this that I ... apologise to Irish women on behalf of what has been predominantly a male-dominated, male-driven disgrace."

Nell McCafferty. She is from Derry and came to public notice after her scathing critiques of Irish life and society especially about the role of women and the situation in the North. She is still an important women's voice in Ireland.

257

Marian Finucane. She is a broadcaster and host of a current affairs and women's issues programme on RTE radio called "Liveline."

David Norris. He is a gay activist and senator representing Trinity College and is a regular guest on chat shows. He was openly gay even before 1993 when homosexuality was illegal in Ireland. His accent is interesting as it is a perfect example of the Anglo-Irish accent – almost hyper-correct English.

Connor Cruise O'Brien. An elder statesman and intellectual with strong views on the North including a rabid opposition to Sinn Féin. His conviction that Britain's main hope is to extricate itself from all involvement in the North without actually solving any of the issues is probably true.

Dr Tony Ryan. Owner of GPA the world's biggest airliner leasing company. Patron of the arts, investor in Ryanair, the first airline to compete domestically and internationally with Aer Lingus.

Annie Murphy. The mother of Bishop Eamon Casey's son. She is American but lived in Dublin for a period in the 1970s where she met and carried on an affair with the bishop for some months.

Bibi Baskin. Journalist and television chat show host. A mild mannered and engaging broadcaster whose weekday show travels around the country interviewing locals and highlighting the various towns.

Susan Denham. Ireland's first woman Supreme Court judge and youngest ever member of the Supreme Court.

Gerry Ryan. He started off his career as a radio disc jockey and chat show host and now also appears on television. He hosts shows like "School Around the Corner," a showpiece for primary school children showing off their musical talents and chatting about school. He also hosts one of those television game shows where the losers get covered in slime.

Pat Kenny. Radio chat show host and presenter of a Saturday night talk show on television. His programme is altogether blander than the others and could be seen as the more conservative side of the Irish.

Darina Allen. Cook and television show presenter whose show now goes out on satellite and English television.

Ray McSharry. He rose to world prominence during the 1992 world GATT (General Agreement on Tariff and Trade) talks which he chaired and finally broke out of deadlock by a mixture of persuasion and threat.

Joe O'Connor. Author, journalist and brother of the singer Sinead. He writes a column for the *Sunday Tribune* from his base in London and occasionally reminds the Irish of their funny ways, while simultaneously lambasting the British for their national defects.

Eamon Dunphy. An ex-footballer with reactionary opinions which he is willing to share with anyone who will listen. Often to be heard commentating on football matches but increasingly often sounding off about things in the press and on television.

THE EDUCATION SYSTEM

Ireland has a strong education system which encourages and allows students to continue their education through to a tertiary level. This belies the still prevelant myth of the rural Irish who are bamboozled by any technology which confronts them but old stereotypes die hard even in modern Europe.

Irish politics come into everything, especially education but the following account is a mere description of the types of schooling available without delving into the complications or issues involved.

Primary School

Primary education is mostly denominational in Ireland. In the Republic, primary schools are called National Schools and children begin there at about the age of six. By default they are church run and the vast majority are run by the Catholic Church. Protestant churches also own and finance and direct the running of schools for children of Protestant families. Anyone who falls between these two divisions is free to go to whichever school they like.

The government has an obligation to provide transport to the nearest school of the correct denomination, so a Protestant child can travel as far as the nearest Protestant school and will be given transport. This is rarely an issue with Catholic schools since few children have far to go to get to one. In the rare cases that Catholic schools are full, Catholic children may attend the local Protestant school in which case they will receive religious education from their priest at the weekend.

Secondary School

At the age of twelve or thirteen, children move on to secondary education which is also largely denominational. At this level Protestant schools are rarer so there is more of a mix in the classrooms. Many schools take little account of this though, offering Catholic doctrine lessons on the timetable while Protestants must make shift for themselves. Attendance at Irish classes is compulsory but it is no longer a compulsory examination subject which means that Irish teachers must deal with a lot of disinterested pupils, perhaps harming those that wish to learn.

The secondary schools offer two types of education – the vocational schools offer a more practical timetable with lots of work related courses and are intended for the less academically inclined while the secondary schools have a more academic bias. In many cases the vocational schools are now better staffed and equipped than the secondaries and are attracting more able pupils. At age fifteen students do a first set of public exams called the Junior Certificate and the results of those exams determine how they progress from there. They may leave school at that stage but few do. At seventeen a second set of exams test students again, known as the Leaving Certificate, and the results of these tests determine a student's chances of entering a tertiary institution.

In Northern Ireland education is even more sectarian with few Catholic and Protestant children mixing at all. The state schools in this case are Protestant while the Catholic Church receives subsidies towards the running of its own schools. Pupils take GCSE exams at the ages of sixteen and eighteen. Universities are nonsectarian and it is here that many young Northern Irish people first experience contact with their previously segregated neighbours. Irish was definitely not on the timetable at schools until quite recently since it has long been associated with the Republicans.

In addition to the state schools, which are free, there are many private schools of all degrees of competence and cost, the most prestigious being Clongowes Wood College where some big names in politics and the arts were educated. Most private schools are run by religious orders and are single sex establishments. There are also, in the Republic, a few community schools, so called because they have a less religious bias and are generally bigger. They are often brought about by the amalgamation of two smaller establishments on a new green field site.

Most of Ireland's immigrants are European and for anyone choosing to settle in the country education with all its religious overtones can present a problem. Choices are between the religious denomination of the schools and whether to send the child to a private school, in which case they may well have to board, or a public one. It is unlikely that children would face any difficulty over religion at school but they may be asked questions which they are best advised to answer with the inquisitive nature of the Irish in mind, rather than with a defensive attitude.

Getting a place in the school you finally opt for is a question of availability of places and the school's acceptance of the pupil. The more prestigious schools may have an entrance examination. In the smaller towns your choices will be very limited unless you send your child to board at a private school. For Japanese people who choose to bring their children to Ireland there is a Japanese school in Kildare which is discussed in chapter twelve.

TRANSPORT

Ireland has an efficient bus system which is fairly inexpensive and well organised with modern buses. There is a railway system although it is not very extensive but a train journey can be an interesting way to see the Irish countryside. Trains run from Cork to Dublin stopping at various towns on the way. Another line runs from Dublin to Tralee in the southwest, while a third goes due west to Mayo. There is a rail link between Dublin and Belfast from where two other lines service the North.

Flights to Ireland are fairly expensive, as are internal flights, but you can obtain a discounted rate which should cost around I£75 for a return fare between Dublin and London. Fares can be as much as double this price unless you can take advantage of the discounted fares.

Dublin, Belfast, Cork and Shannon are more or less international standard airports. Flights can be made from around thirteen cities in the United Kingdom and direct international flights are available from the United States, and around sixteen European cities including Moscow. Remember that it may be necessary to say a Hail Mary or two on approach at the captain's request, so remember to pack a prayer book!

Several ferries and jetfoils link Ireland with England and France although they are best avoided, being arduously long and badly designed. The weather and seas between England and Ireland can be quite severe at times and are sometimes a real test of one's sea legs.

Within the country most people travel by private car. Roads are good near to the big cities but get smaller and more like country lanes the further out of town you go. When driving in rural Ireland be prepared for possible delays caused by livestock being moved or even just some locals who may have stopped for a quick chat as they pass each other.

Taxis are available in most big towns and the usual car hire companies also have offices around the country. Cars are very expensive compared to prices in England. Many companies around Ireland find it profitable to import used cars from Japan to sell on the second-hand market.

CULTURAL QUIZ

There are very few situations that occur in Ireland where the intrepid world traveller cannot get by with a bit of ingenuity. Irish people love strangers and their funny ways. But here are a few situations you may find a little difficult to deal with as a newcomer. See if you know the best way to handle them.

SITUATION 1

You employ a small local firm to do a building job around your house. After several arrangements for starting dates have come and gone, a man turns up in an old van, does some of the work and disappears. A week or so later a different man turns up, finishes the work and goes off saying not to worry about payment because the boss will see to it and he will send you a bill for payment of the work. After a few weeks no bill arrives. Do you:

A   Send a cheque in the post for the estimated cost.
B   Forget about it.
C   Phone up to remind them that they've not sent a bill.
D   Remember vaguely what the estimate was and keep some cash handy.

Comment

Actually any or all of these options are fine. People are very relaxed and trusting in Ireland about getting paid for things. They know where you are so why worry about getting paid? A bill will arrive eventually or the builder might show up out of the blue for the cash, or you might bump into him in the street.

The most Irish response is D. Everybody prefers cash payments rather than cheques. In the cities a builder might be a bit more efficient about collecting payments and giving receipts.

C would be very un-Irish and would be a cause for humour. It isn't likely to produce any response though.

A could well cause confusion and wouldn't be done by an Irish person.

If you chose B then you might get a sudden shock two months later when you finally get asked for payment.

SITUATION 2

You have just moved into a small town and wish to endear yourself to the locals. The obvious place to do so is in the local pub. You go in and settle down at the bar. Do you then:

A Offer to stand everyone a drink.

B Wait till someone begins a conversation with you.

C Latch on to the most likely looking character and crack a joke about the government.

D Ask the bar keeper about interesting local places to visit.

Comment

Here there are several wrong responses, depending on where the village is, whether or not you are English and what sex you are. If you are a woman, going into the pub may get people talking to you immediately but may also get you a reputation as a fast women. If the village is in Northern Ireland or perhaps even one of the border counties politics is absolutely out as a topic of conversation. Also if you are English you can easily rouse some resentment with the wrong comments about Irish life.

Option A, of standing everyone a drink, is costly in a country where a pint of Guinness costs almost I£2 and will win immediate friends but probable contempt as someone who is too free with their money.

Option B is usually a safe bet but may not get an immediate response and may label you unfriendly.

Option D has to be the best response of all. It provides a neutral topic, allows the bar person and anyone else interested to give advice, which people love to do, and opens up the conversation for the chief topic of interest which is you and how long you are going to be there, where you come from, where you work etc., etc., etc.

SITUATION 3

You have arranged to buy some furniture from a small but classy furniture store some distance from where you live. They have given you a date for delivery. The date goes by and a telephone call discovers that there are technical problems in the delivery. Several more dates go by. Do you:

A   Cancel the order.
B   Phone up, demand to speak to the manager and have a raving fit.
C   Keep on reminding them pleasantly by phone that your furniture has not yet arrived.
D   Wait.

Comment

Option A will just make you angry, frustrated and furniture-less. You'll have to find another shop, reorder and maybe go through the whole process again.

Option B may well be successful in getting your order but it won't be at all the Irish way of doing things. The person you talk to won't understand your anger and will only shake their head and mutter 'foreigner' to whoever is with them on the other end of the phone line.

Option C is probably the most rewarding and educational choice. You'll get lots of good excuses for the delay as well as learn to control your temper.

D is risky since there is always the chance that the order might never come at all. Whichever option you choose the stuff is probably going to get there eventually, at its own speed and why bother having a fit or getting excited over it? You've lived all this time without it so a little longer won't matter.

SITUATION 4

You go into a local butcher's shop to pick up some meat. When you enter the butcher is chatting with a customer who is already in the shop. You smile, reassuring yourself that the lifestyle is so relaxed here that nobody rushes. Then an old lady comes in and addresses the butcher, who breaks off his conversation and gets her a chair. She sits down and the three of them are set for a ten minute discussion of lumbago, the doctor, Siobhan's confirmation and last weeks stillborn calf. Do you:

A Join in enthusiastically with your own lumbago problems.
B Wait.
C Go to the supermarket.
D Say, "Excuse me, I was here first, can I have some service?"

Comment

Answer A is what any Irish person would do. If you stay out of the conversation you are the peculiar one, not the others. They are not ignoring you because you have every right to join in for what may turn into some good crack.

Answer B is also good. They won't leave you waiting for long and the butcher will probably realise that you don't want to talk and will attend to you while he carries on with the conversation.

If you choose C and go to the supermarket there is no guarantee that the same thing won't happen there – twice, once at the meat counter and again at the check-out!

Answer D will get you what you want but is not recommended as a way of making friends.

SITUATION 5

You are a woman who has recently moved to Ireland and you are eagerly awaiting the arrival of some important documents which are being delivered by courier. The courier van drives up and a man calls at the door and says, "Is the boss in?" Do you:

A   Calmly explain that you do not have a boss in your house and that being a grown up it is OK for you to receive the package.

B   Give him a five minute lecture on how women are considered the equals of men in the rest of the world and accuse him of sexism.

C   Smile coquettishly and say: "No, will I do?"

D   Inform him that he is already speaking to the boss.

Comment

Option C is the only one that the indigenous MCP will understand. He won't even have noticed what he was saying, let alone think it may have irritated/ annoyed/ amused/ confused you. You may later engage in debate about bosses and male/female relationships in Ireland and he will be perfectly charming and interested in talking about it. This will not, however, prevent him from saying the same thing at the next house he calls at.

A and B will draw a complete blank since all he wants to do is make his delivery.

D is the nicest way of answering because it at once rebukes him for his attitude and laughs at him in true Irish slagging style.

FURTHER READING

All paperback unless otherwise stated.

Maps

There is no shortage of quality maps. *The Mitchelin Map of Ireland* No 405 (1:1,000,000) has the scenic roads highlighted in green.

The four maps that make up the *Ordnance Survey Holiday Map* series (1:250,000) are very useful if something more detailed than a whole country map is needed.

For greater detail the Ordnance Survey covers the whole island in 25 sheets with a 1:126,720 scale (half an inch to one mile). This series is currently being replaced by an excellent new series of 89 maps with a 1:50,000 scale (two centimetres to one kilometre). For a local area there is no better map.

Travel Guides

Just about every travel guide publisher in the world has brought out an Ireland title. The best of the lot is the second edition of *Ireland: Travel Survival Kit*, S. Sheehan, T. Smallman and P. Yale, Lonely Planet Publications 1996.

Another good guide is *Ireland: The Rough Guide*, M. Greenwood and H. Hawkins, Penguin London 1994.

More detailed guidebooks include:

The Insider's Guide to Kerry and West Cork, P. Levy and S. Sheehan, Gill and Macmillan Dublin 1995 and;

Dublin: City Guide, T. Smallman, Lonely Planet Publications 1996.

The best way to see Ireland and meet people is by walking and cycling the countryside. *The Irish Cycling Guide*, B. Walsh, Gill and Macmillan

Dublin 1994, is a set of suggested tours with details of distances and types of road.

The best local walking guide is the *New Irish Walk Guides*, Gill and Macmillan Dublin 1993.

The *Bridgestone Guides*, J and S. McKenna, Estragon Durrus, County Cork include; *100 Best Places to Stay in Ireland*, *100 Best Places to Eat in Ireland*, *100 Best Restaurants in Ireland* and *Vegetarians' Guide to Ireland*.

Archaeology, Architecture and Art

Heritage – A Visitor's Guide, E. Brennan (ed.) Office of Public Works Dublin 1993, is a useful introduction to the antiquities looked after by the Office of Public Works. They also issue a I£15 'Heritage Card' which gives access to all the various castles and other sites under their control.

Archaeological Inventory of County Cork, Volume 1 – West Cork, D. Power et al (eds.) Office of Public Works Dublin 1993, is an example of the kind of detailed exploration that is possible in the Irish countryside. Nearly 500 pages make up this archaeological inventory of West Cork and at I£20 in hardback this is exceptional value. Maps locate every site recorded, including megalithic tombs, stone circles, bolder-burials, standing stones, prehistoric copper mines, pit and urn burials, abbeys and post-medieval military and industrial sites.

Irish Treasures is the name of a useful series of inexpensive books published by Town House in 1995 and includes *Early Irish Monasteries* by C. Manning, which looks at the surviving monastic monuments, from the elaborate high crosses and tiny dry-stone oratories to larger churches and round towers.

In the same series, *Stone Circles in Prehistoric Ireland*, S. Nualláin, is an illustrated and informative account of the subject.

Early Celtic Art in Ireland, E. Kelly, Town House Dublin 1993, is a general introduction with black and white illustrations.

Music

Books of Irish ballads are available in every bookshop in Ireland.

Ballads from the Pubs of Ireland, J. Healy (ed.) Mercier Press Cork 1992, is in three little volumes and they contain varied selections of the country's traditional melancholy and merry lyrics.

Folk Music and Dances of Ireland, Breandan Breathnach, Mercier Press Cork 1992, studies the history and present state of Irish traditional music, song and dance.

Irish Rock, M. Prendergast, O'Brien Press Dublin 1993 and *Irish Rock*, T. Clayton-Lea and R. Taylor, Gill and Macmillan Dublin 1993 both chronicle Ireland's continuing contribution to the world of rock and popular music.

Cooking

Traditional Irish Recipes, G. Thompson, O'Brien Press Dublin 1990, and *Irish Traditional Food*, T. Fitzgibbon, Gill and Macmillan Dublin 1991, are two useful books to get started with. There is also *The Irish Cookbook,* C. Blake, Mercier Press Cork 1991.

A number of renowned Irish chefs have published some of their recipes and two of the best collections are to be found in *Myrtle Allen's Cooking at Ballymaloe*, M. Allen, Gill and Macmillan Dublin 1992 and *Irish Bistro Cooking*, M. Clifford, Mercier Press Cork 1993.

Cooking with Irish Spirits, M. Johnson, Wolfhound Press Dublin 1995, explains how to put a kick into food with the help of Irish spirits, beer and even poteen.

Ireland 1996, Macmillan London 1996, is the *Egon Ronay Gourmet Guide* to Ireland and a new edition is usually published each year.

Genealogy

Heraldic Artists are a Dublin publisher (3, Nassau St, Dublin 2) who specialise in books on the tracing of one's Irish roots. Their *Irish Genealogy: A Record Finder* explains how and where to find records of ancestors and their *Family Tree: Ancestral Record* is a self-indexing pocket book to record your family tree.

Irish Family Histories, I. Grehan, Town House Dublin 1995, has nearly 300 pages on the origins and history of over 200 family names.

Tracing Your Irish Ancestors: A Comprehensive Guide, J. Grenham, Gill and Macmillan Dublin 1992, is another practical guide dealing with the subject.

History

The Green Flag, R. Kee, Penguin 1986, consists of three volumes that offer a highly readable narrative of Irish history up to the creation of the Free State.

Maud Gonne, Margaret Wood, Harper Collins London 1992, is one of a series of Pandora books dealing with the life and times of Irish women in the nationalist struggle. The same series includes *Constance Markievicz* by Anne Havery (1988).

For post-1922 history, *Ireland: A Social and Cultural History,* T. Brown, Fontana London 1986, offers an unsentimental analysis of the important issues.

The Long War, Brendan O'Brien, O'Brien Press Dublin 1995, is an updated paperback version of a book exploring the development of the IRA and Sinn Féin up to the talks that led to the IRA ceasefire.

The classic study of the 1845–49 famine is *The Great Hunger*, C. Woodham-Smith, Hamilton London 1985. Liam O'Flaherty used the catastrophe as the basis for his novel *Famine*, Wolfhound Press Dublin 1988.

A History of Ulster, J. Bardon, Blackstaff Press Belfast 1992, is a big book that starts with prehistory and works its way through the Troubles. The sad tale is told in a highly readable manner that manages to be scrupulously fair.

A Generation of Violence, J. Bowyer-Bell, Gill and Macmillan Dublin 1993 – the title tells the story.

Proved Innocent, Gerry Conlon, Penguin London 1990, tells the tale of the awful miscarriage of justice as result of the British justice system's ruthless determination to make sure people were convicted for IRA bombing outrages in England during the 1970s and later. The film version, *In the Name of the Father*, is also worth viewing.

Politics

It's difficult to recommend a good book about contemporary Irish politics, mainly due to the subject's inherent boredom, and the one book that is readable is now unfortunately out of print. The book, *The Begrudger's Guide to Irish Politics*, by B. O'Heithir, is well worth seeking out in a library or second-hand bookshop.

Gerry Adams, the president of Sinn Féin, gives an informative and convincing account of the Republican point of view in *The Politics of Irish Freedom*, Brandon Books Tralee 1986.

Highly recommended is *Selected Writings*, Gerry Adams, Brandon Books Tralee 1994.

Paisley, E. Moloney and A. Pollack, Poolbeg Books Dublin 1986, is a fascinating account of the rise to power of the leader of the Democratic Unionist Party and the Free Presbyterian Church of Ulster. The book is worth reading just for the shocking Paisley speech that is quoted in the Introduction.

Anatomy of a Changing State, Gemma Hussey, Penguin London 1995, tells the story of Irish cultural and political life up to 1993 and is a very readable, if occasionally superficial, account of contemporary life in Ireland.

The Anglo-Irish Experience

The best insight into the unique Anglo-Irish world is provided in *Woodbrook,* D. Thomson, Penguin London 1994. As a young man Thomson came to the northwest as a tutor to an Anglo-Irish family and his book charts his gradual awakening to the reality around him.

Hungry Hill, Daphne du Maurier, Penguin London 1965, is a novel based fairly closely on the history of an Anglo-Irish family who owned the once valuable copper mines at the end of the Beara Peninsula in West Cork. Daphne du Maurier had access to the family papers and blends fact with fiction.

Literature

You would require a few years left alone in a university library to work through the classics of literature in English written by Irish men and women. Jonathan Swift (1667–1745), William Congreve (1670–1729), George Farquhar (1678–1707), Laurence Sterne (1713–68), Oliver Goldsmith (1728–74), R. B. Sheridan (1751–1816), George Bernard Shaw (1856–1950), W. B. Yeats (1856–1939), John Millington Synge (1871–1909), Sean O'Casey (1880–1964) and James Joyce (1882–1941) are just some of the more famous names born before 1900. One of the greatest of all, Samuel Beckett, was born in 1906 and died in 1989.

James Joyce, although he died over fifty years ago, is still essential reading for anyone wishing to engage with Irish culture. The collection of short stories *Dubliners*, Penguin London 1994, is the best introduction, followed by *A Portrait of the Artist as a Young Man*, Penguin London 1994, a largely autobiographical tale of a young man coming to realise his artistic vocation and the need to employ 'silence, exile and cunning' in his battle against the Catholic Church and other native forms of oppression.

For a taste of Irish humour at its most anarchic and metaphysical there are no better books than those written by Flann O'Brien, real name Brian O'Nolan, who also used the glorious pseudonym Myles na Gopaleen. His novels like *The Third Policeman*, *At Swim-Two-Birds* and *The Dalkey Archive* are all published by Penguin Books.

Flann O'Brien died in 1966 but the comic tradition is being well preserved by the Dubliner Roddy Doyle. In 1993 he won the Booker

Prize for his *Paddy Clarke Ha Ha Ha*. Earlier *The Commitments* was made into a successful film – which is well worth viewing – and *The Snapper* and *The Van*, published by Penguin, traces the difficult times of the same family.

Contemporary Irish fiction is alive and kicking. *Deep End*, G. Philpott, Poolbeg Dublin 1994, is a novel dealing with AIDS and *Stir-Fry*, E. Donoghue, Penguin London 1993, deals with the issue of lesbianism in Ireland.

There is also a strong literary tradition in Northern Ireland. *Cal*, B. MacLaverty, Penguin London 1983 and *Lies of Silence,* B. Moore, Penguin London 1990, are both interesting novels that focus on the grim environment in the North.

A useful collection of contemporary poetry may be found in *Contemporary Irish Poetry*, P. Fallon and J. Mahon (eds.) Penguin London 1990 and it includes work by Seamus Heaney – the most famous living Irish poet.

Finally, *A Dictionary of Irish Quotations*, Mercier Press Cork 1994 and *The Sayings of James Joyce*, Duckworth London 1995, both by S. Sheehan are worth dipping into for their examples of the Irish way with words.

THE AUTHOR

Pat Levy is a teacher and author who divides her time between the bustle of Hong Kong and the more sublime lifestyle of West Cork in the Republic of Ireland. She has written a number of books dealing with the cultures of various countries, including *The Insiders Guide to Kerry and West Cork.*

Her experience as a frequent visitor and sometime resident of the country has allowed her to gain an insight into the vagaries of Irish life and which she is glad to be able to share with the readers of *Culture Shock! Ireland.* Her hope is that the book will dispel many of the myths which surround Ireland and its people and that the reader's stay will be enriched by getting beneath the surface and discovering the real Ireland.

INDEX

Abortion   83, 179–180
Adams, Gerry   16, 75-76, 78
Agriculture   136–137
Anglo-Irish War   41

Battle of the Boyne   30, 68
Begrudgery   105–106
Blarney Castle   14
Blarney, Lord   13
Bloody Sunday   73
Blow-ins   54, 217
Brehon Law   26
Business Hours   149
Business Methods   151

Casey, Bishop   19, 174
Censorship   194–195, 203
Chauvinism   114
Church
   attendance   87
   in daily life   89
Class divisions   218–219
Contraception   176–178
Crack   49–50, 55
Currency   109

Dáil   42, 50
Dancing   191
De Valera, Eamon   23, 42, 102
Divorce   180–182
Downing Street Declara-
      tion   74, 78, 81

Dress   240
Drinking   12, 126–133
   see also pubs
Driving   236–237, 263

Ecumenism   100
Education system   259–262
Emigration   163–167
English
   invasion by   26
Ethnic groups   205–220
   Indians   214–215
   Anglo Irish   220
   Chinese   212–213
   Europeans   216–217
   Japanese   216
   Jews   209–211
   Muslims   211–212
   Travellers   206–209
European Union (EU)   136, 182–
      184, 206

Fairy forts   96
Falls Road   82
Famine   35
Festivals
   calender of events   251–253
   modern   193
   traditional   192
Film industry   196–197
Food   117–123
   dining out   126
   traditional   122

Free Derry 82
Funerals 91

Gaelic
    football 55
    language 14, 26, 59–64
Gaelic Athletic Association
        (GAA) 227–228
Gaelic Revival 38
Gaeltacht 61
Genealogy 168–171
Geography 255
Guinness 131

History 23–47
Holy days 90
Home Rule 37–38
Homes
    city 157
    country 159–160
    stately 161–162
Hospitality 124–125

Immigration 205–206
Industries 136–143
IRA (Irish Republican Army) 16,
        68, 72, 74–75
Irish Parliament *see* Dáil

Jackeen 55
Joyce, James 38, 108, 211, 238

Land
    attachment to 153
Language 49–65
    accents 64
    basic vocabulary 54–57
    Irish English 50
Literature 194–196
Lotto 107
Luck money 108

Maastricht Treaty 184
Media
    newspapers 200–202
    radio 199–200
    restrictions 202
    television 198–199
Money
    attitudes to 103
    displays of wealth 110
Moving statues 98–100
Music 189–191

Northern Ireland 68–82

O'Connell, Daniel 34
Office hours 250

Paisley, Ian 65, 70, 78
Penal Laws 31–33
Pilgrimage 89
Pishogues 56, 95–97

Plantation   28–29
Politics, summary of   246–250
Postal services   253
Potatoes   117–119
Prices   108
Priesthood   93, 174
Provisional IRA   75
Public holidays   250
Public toilets   240
Pubs   12, 126–130
    etiquette   130
Puck Fair   96

Religion   86–101
RUC (Royal Ulster Constabu-
    lary)   72

Safety
    in public   245–246
Shankill Road   82
Sinn Féin   16, 76, 249
Skellig lists   95
Slagging   50
Sport and leisure   223–235
    boxing   227
    fife and drum bands   235
    fishing   231–233
    greyhound racing   226
    horse racing   223–226
    hurling   229–230
    road bowling   230
    seaside   233
    soccer   235–236

St. Patrick   23, 89
St. Patrick's Day   90
Statutes of Kilkenny   28
Stereotypes   10–18
Stormont   68, 81

Taioseach   42, 50, 63
Taxation   111
Television   256
Time   254
Tourism   138–141, 185–186
Transport   262

UFF (Ulster Freedom Fight-
    ers)   77
Ulster   29–30, 40, 42, 73
Unemployment   143–145

Visiting etiquette   243

Wakes   91, 97
Weddings   91, 244
Weights and measures   254
Whiskey   133
Women
    attitudes to   113
    role of   67
Work ethic   135

Yeats, W. B.   22, 83